······· The ·······
ROOKIE
MOM'S
Handbook

By HEATHER GIBBS FLETT and WHITNEY MOSS

The
ROOKIE
MOM'S
Handbook

250 ACTIVITIES
to do with (and without!)
your baby

QUIRK BOOKS
PHILADELPHIA

Library of Congress Cataloging in Publication Number: 2007937179

ISBN: 978-1-59474-219-4

Printed in China
Typeset in Goudy, New Baskerville, Matrix, and Phosphate
Designed by Becky Berkheimer
Illustrations by Amy Saidens
Edited by Melissa Wagner

Distributed in North America by Chronicle Books
680 Second Street
San Francisco, CA 94107

10 9 8 7 6 5 4 3 2 1

Quirk Books
215 Church Street
Philadelphia, PA 19106
www.quirkbooks.com

Disclaimer: This book is not meant to take the place of advice
from a qualified medical professional.

Contents

1 ★ *INTRODUCTION*

9 ★ **TAKING BABY STEPS** ★

From pretending you're in Paris to getting fit at baby boot camp

11 ★ *Month 1*

27 ★ *Month 2*

45 ★ *Month 3*

61 ★ **ROLLING OVER (AND ROLLING WITH IT)** ★

From enjoying modern art to your first weekend getaway

63 ★ *Month 4*

77 ★ *Month 5*

93 ★ *Month 6*

109 ★ **LEARNING TO CRAWL** ★

From the farmer's market to swapping for new clothes

111 ★ *Month 7*

127 ★ *Month 8*

145 ★ *Month 9*

161 ★ **NOW WE'RE CRUISING** ★

From test-driving music classes to launching Camp Grandma

163 ★ *Month 10*

177 ★ *Month 11*

191 ★ *Month 12*

207 ★ *ROOKIE MOMS MILESTONES*

210 ★ *RECOMMENDED READING*

212 ★ *INDEX*

216 ★ *ACKNOWLEDGMENTS*

Introduction

WELCOME TO MOTHERHOOD!

For the purposes of this book, let's assume that this is also a welcome to maternity leave. Not working—whether it's for six weeks, six months, or six years—is going to change your life. Of course, that little person you have to take care of is going to make your life pretty different as well. But we're here to talk about you.

It's your first time, right? You're a rookie mom. Untrained, no experience. That's you. And that's not an insult.

Even those of us who spent our adolescence babysitting for other people's children or who work as preschool teachers or pediatric nurses are in for some big surprises. We've never been moms before. It's not the same as changing a few diapers or setting up messy art projects. It means you are in charge all day, every day, and you and that baby are not going anywhere (or getting out of pajamas) unless you make it happen.

When our babies were born, we discovered that hours and days lose shape when you have no place you're expected to be. For those of us who are accustomed to a scheduled, busy life, that can be confusing. Lack of structure can throw even the most confident, opinionated woman into a state of mental uncertainty.

We know one rookie mom who actually had to pronounce 8 P.M. as an artificial bedtime, by which hour the newborn should be put in his pajamas. If he was still wearing clothes at 9 P.M., she would freak out at her husband and hiss "Pajamas!" Why? Because she needed structure. It didn't matter that the baby was going to sleep on and off in seemingly eternal cycles. Daytime was for clothes and nighttime for pajamas, even for her 5-week-old baby!

No matter how fulfilling you may find motherhood, it's awfully quiet if done in isolation, and it can be pretty disorienting to have your whole day as a blank slate. We can assure you that counting the hours until your partner comes home is not going to make the time pass quickly. Whether you're home all day with baby or only seeing him after work and on weekends, sometimes it's hard to know what to do with this little person who doesn't talk or walk. Your baby's not going to say, "Hey, mom, let's go to the coffee shop and get you a treat!" You're going to have to come up with ideas all by yourself.

That's where this book enters the scene. Inside is some help in creating your own structure. We have assembled 250 activities that we enjoyed doing ourselves. Some are crafty, some are adventurous, and some are just a way to help you get a meal on the table. All of them can be done by someone with a baby. Pick an activity each morning and build your day around it.

We won't ask you to be capable of much during the first month. We know you're exhausted, nervous, and, of course, still recovering from giving birth. Mostly you should be resting when possible. But, as your confidence builds (yes, yes it will!), we'll suggest some more challenging outings. As you read, take a peek at the later months to preview how much fun you'll be having as your baby gets older.

GET OUT OF THE HOUSE!

No matter what activity you choose, we are adamant that you must get out of the house, even when it seems easier just to stay in. The baby will be less fussy, and you'll be happier, too.

That is your responsibility each day. When all the other adults leave the house and you're there alone with that kid, you *must* commit to some outing that will take you outside. Your activity can be as small as driving to the mall, where you will be forced to change a diaper in a public restroom. Good for you! That's what moms do, and you're learning to do it.

Are you out of orange juice? Go to the store and buy some. We're telling you to go to the store just for one thing? Yes! If that's what will give you purpose and practice with taking your child somewhere, that's what you should do.

Not every activity in this book is an outing. Some are crafts or things to do while your baby sleeps. Here's your homework: If an activity sounds good to you, figure out how you're going to do it—*and* leave the house—all in one day! We know it's hard, and we're here to encourage you.

Throughout the book, we also suggest some strategies for getting mom-alone time and mom-hangs-with-friend time because mama, you need that, too.

7 REASONS TO LEAVE THE HOUSE EACH DAY

1   It's an excuse to take a shower.

2   It's an opportunity to show off your baby.

3   It will help you maintain your friendships.

4   It will help keep your social skills sharp.

5   You'll actually have something to say when you're asked, "What did you do all day?"

6   You can practice using your baby gear (until you can do it with one hand).

7   That's what people do, and moms are just people who have children.

WHY THIS BOOK?

Before having babies, we had this image of what motherhood would look and feel like. We wanted to be laid-back, cool parents. We imagined a life in which we dressed ourselves in cute clothes and spent our days cuddling a smiling baby. But it wasn't that way at all. Instead, we were paralyzed with fear, obsessed with sleep training, feeling fat, and unable to sustain a conversation.

We think that all first-timers experience some or all of those feelings and ultimately discover their own coping strategies. Ours was to find activities and outings to help us get unstuck and prove that we could enjoy things while toting babies along. We wrote this book to provide ideas for rookie moms to get out and have more fun. For new mothers, sometimes it's hard to think (admit it, you agree). Sometimes it's just nice to be told what to do. Here we are. We're telling you.

When we met, Kurt Cobain was already dead, but people our age were still dressing like him. Many years and a couple of overpriced bridesmaids dresses later, our shared obstetrician literally left newly pregnant Heather waist-down naked on the exam table to run to the hospital to be with past-due pregnant Whitney waist-down naked on the delivery table.

In the months that followed, we shared the experience of first-time motherhood, learning about our new sons and also our new selves.

.... *About Heather (as told by Whitney)* ....

This crazy chick used to track guests in an Excel spreadsheet *during* her parties. Now she has two cutie-pie sons and a cutie-pie husband, all of whom may go crazy over the next 65 years as she enters their every move into a spreadsheet. Heather recorded 8 months' worth of data about baby Holden's eating habits for her reviewing pleasure.

For some reason, when Heather saw me in the hospital after my son was born, even though I felt like I had been run over by a truck, she thought, "That looks like fun!" When I went to visit her after her son was born, I asked if she felt like she had been run over by a truck.

She looked at me with shock and asked how I knew — and what else had I forgotten to tell her? I would like to put in writing that I did not forget to tell her anything. She forgot to write it all down.

P.S. Things have gotten much, much better since then.

About Whitney (as told by Heather)

Whitney is crafty, fun, stylish, and original. She is always up for some creative handmade project. She impressed me with her knit caps from the first day we met, but it wasn't until she had a room full of "normal" people decorating onesies with fabric paint, stencils, and stickers at my baby shower that I knew she could bring out the creativity in all of us. I left that day with a stack of onesies-of-a-kind. (Can I say that?)

Whitney inspires me to be a better mom and have fun along the way. It's true I have selective amnesia about how hard it all may be for her. . . . I only noticed the smiles and laughter in between her baby Julian's tears. When my husband went back to work after my own son was born, Whit took the day off from her job to teach me the mysterious ways of life on maternity leave. She took me on my first outing to the grocery store, made me lunch, ordered me out of my ill-fitting maternity jeans, and helped me take a nap. What a woman!

Taking Baby Steps

MONTHS 1 THROUGH 3

Wow. You did it: You made a person. Nice work, lady. Or should we say "mama"?

But if you thought that was the finish line, you're in for a rude awakening. And likely not just one awakening . . . but several per night! While you wonder if you'll ever feel like your old self again, you'll just have to fake it for a while. You're on an emotional roller coaster, and that's totally normal.

············ YOUR NEW SKILLS ············

* Swaddling a baby
* Using a stroller, a car seat, and maybe even a front carrier
* Holding someone with a wobbly head

············ YOUR NEW FEARS ············

* Your body has been permanently damaged
* You'll never see your friends again
* You're not a real mom
* You're doing it all wrong

You are going to be OK. The hormones will subside, the belly will recede, and your partner will stick through it with you. Think back to when you were 8 weeks old. That's right: Your baby will not remember any of this, either! The wee one is extremely portable right now. You can go wherever you want and take your sidekick with you—even movie theaters, dinner parties, and scenic hikes. Take it one day at a time, and you'll get comfortable doing more and more adventurous things. Baby steps, girlfriend.

#1 Take "baby" steps and get out of the house.

Whitney's retelling of her first days at home after birth always includes, "I could barely walk." Some of us can barely walk — and some of us can barely sit. It really depends on which part of your body the baby damaged on her way out. Though we want you to think of us as your friends, and as such we extend our sympathy to your sore parts, we also want to push you to get on with your life. This is because we love you.

Take walks outside with your new stroller to get some air. Most babies respond well to the rhythm of the stroller, the fresh air, and the changing light. C-section sisters, no brisk walking for you, but you do need to get outside. Have someone take you and your little bundle to a place other than your house for a change of scenery.

Also, don't push yourself too hard the first month. Heather's first walk was two blocks. Literally. One out, one back. Take it easy.

#2 Get to know your gear.

We recommend that you try using that new baby carrier, stroller, *whatever* before you really need it.

Imagine driving someplace for the first time alone with your baby and realizing upon arrival that you didn't learn how to open and collapse the stroller. Oops. You'll be sweating and swearing in the parking lot, hoping that a kindhearted veteran parent will happen by and save you. Don't let that be your fate.

Whitney actually hooked up the 17 interlocking parts of her electric breast pump and practiced using it on her thigh when she was 40 weeks pregnant. It was a good thing, too: She ended up really needing to use it the day after she gave birth, which is no time to figure out such an appliance.

What unfamiliar gear is in your arsenal? Do you know the function of each button on your swing? Wouldn't it be great if all the batteries worked?

#3 Hydrate from your own bottle.

Are you drinking enough water? Keep track of how many ounces you drink today. Try to get to 96 (almost three liters!). Nursing, sleeplessness, or regular old postpartum recovery can feel like an unending hangover. You need lots of water to get over it. Start chugging now.

#4 *Free your hands.*

We each have at least three different ways to carry our baby hands-free (soft front carriers, ring slings, pouches, lengthy wraps, and backpacks for bigger babies), but we agree that the easiest for a new mom is the BabyBjörn. There's less questioning whether you're "doing it right." Unlike some of the crazy fabric sheaths that are sold as infant carriers,* the BabyBjörn is a symmetrical device that fits snugly against you. You may come to think of it as your new best friend.

············ **HERE ARE SOME TIPS TO HELP YOU ON YOUR WAY** ············

★ **Practice taking the BabyBjörn on and off.** This is best attempted when your baby doesn't need a ride—preferably when she's safely sleeping in her bassinet or in someone else's arms rather than in your own.

★ **If you get stuck, look at the little picture on the inside to show you what to do.** Or read the instructions online.

★ **When installing the baby, remember:** Itty-bitty babies face you, and babies with good head control face the world.

★ **If you're wearing it correctly, you should be able to kiss the top of your baby's head with a simple nod.**

★ **Put a little hat on the baby to protect her brand-new, delicate skin from the sun.**

★ **Put on your own jacket to look really advanced.**

---

* Note: If you had a C-section, you might not be ready to use this piece of gear for a few weeks. Use these tips to get your partner strapped up instead.

#5 *Just say "NO."*

Juggling a new baby and your shifting identity is time consuming. Are there any little (or big) obligations that you can let slide? Let them.

Use your new status as a chance to say no without guilt and relish the feeling of relief when you tell someone "no" when you usually would have said, "Sure, I can do that."

You'll be tackling seemingly endless tasks again before you know it, anyway. Enjoy a break from them while you can!

#6 *Call your grandma.*

If you have any living grandmothers, call one and ask about her childbirth experiences. Some parts might sound horrific (no partner in the room, maybe no pain relief, or worse, knocked out entirely), but some might sound lovely. (We're not sure what. Let us know if you hear anything good!)

Nana's story will mean more to you now than it did before, and obviously she will be thrilled to hear from you.

#7 *Increase your calcium the fun way.*

According to the National Dairy Council, women over age 18 should consume about 1,000 mg of calcium per day. That works out to about 3 servings, the equivalent of 2 venti vanilla lattes.

We hope you've already realized that this book is not the place to read about counting calories or shedding pounds. We want you to be happy, not weight obsessed, while you adjust to your new baby—so we gladly recommend the following 7 tasty ways to get your daily dose:

1 **Mint chocolate chip ice cream** in front of the TV

2 **Cheese** (fancy, with a little red wine, or the stick variety in the middle of the night)

3 **A tall glass of milk,** with cookies or cake

4 **Hot chocolate** made with real milk

5 **Decaf latte** (single shot, double tall)

6 **Real whipped cream** on anything

7 **Almond-flavored steamed milk** from that sexy barista

#8 *Write a "did do" list.*

If you're getting sick of your "to do" list getting longer rather than shorter and wondering where the heck all your time is going, try writing a "did do" list. Share it with your baby-daddy at the end of the day and encourage him to be very impressed. The truth is that your time is filled with lots and lots of recurring tasks that you never had to deal with before.

So set aside this list:
········· **TO DO** ·········

☐ Fix chip in front windshield
☐ Call Marnie back
☐ Change name with United Airlines
☐ Order wedding albums
☐ Buy Chad's birthday present

For at least one day, make this list:
········· **DID DO** ·········

☑ Changed 2 wet diapers
☑ Changed 4 poopy diapers, 1 blowout
☑ Selected 2 full outfits
☑ Changed baby's entire outfit 3 times
☑ Nursed for 4 hours
☑ Photographed baby asleep on couch
☑ Showered, mostly
☑ Ate breakfast
☑ Made myself lunch; ate half of it
☑ Made this list

You get the idea. Own it. Live it. Love it.

#9 *Put on your own oxygen mask first.*

This is a friendly reminder: You're not doing your baby any favors by overlooking your own needs. When you're awakened in the middle of the night by a screaming, hungry baby, take the extra minute to chug some water, pee, and scarf down some crackers before picking her up. You never know when it's going to turn into a marathon soothing session, and everything seems worse when you're a starving, thirsty lunatic. And if you're still taking pain meds, don't forget them in the middle of the night. Getting out of bed in the morning will be easier if the ibuprofen is already flowing through your system.

Before bed, set up a little aid station to use in the darkest hours of the night.

#10 *Take a nice hot shower.*

Feeling nervous? Your baby's not. The white noise of the shower reminds her of the sounds of your uterus, her old stomping ground. Here's what to do:

1 Put bouncy chair or car seat in bathroom.
2 Secure baby in place.
3 Turn on shower.
4 Remove clothes.
5 Step inside.

#11 Support your breasts (and yourself).

Nobody told you breastfeeding would be so hard, huh? Yeah, we know. It's that way for most of us.

Get thee to a support group. Even if you're not having problems now, you might eventually need help, and it's a good idea to know where to go before you need it. There might be one at your hospital, or look for meetings hosted by La Leche League. (They also give free advice by phone.)

This task is important, worthy of being your first solo outing with the baby. If you want to keep it up, you need a village of support, and there is one out there. You'll find it inspiring to see other nursing moms with their older babies.

If you feel overwhelmed, just drive carefully—you can cry when you get there. It's expected!

#12 Make the best (or worst) swaddling blanket

If making something with your hands is fun for you, and if you also like having a well-rested baby, then this activity is right up your alley.

Buy a 40-square-inch (1-square-meter) piece of flannel printed with a cute pattern, then finish (or hem) the edges. A perfect square makes the best swaddler, but any shape will do for a stroller blanket or play mat—so you're a winner even if it comes out deformed.

#13 *Track your child's every movement.*

For some personality types, geeking out on baby data is an ideal job for the parent who did not give birth. Enough said.

But for the project managers and bossy big sisters among us, counting, tracking, and trying to manage are all part of the job of mothering.

Luckily, there are many tools to help indulge the impulse to obsessively track your baby's every move (and movement): gadgets, Web sites, fun books with cute covers and symbols, and even homegrown spreadsheets. We have one that you can try: Check out the Rookie Moms baby tracker template at www.rookiemoms.com/babytracker.

You may find that you engage in this activity for a short time, like Whitney, who lost interest after the first few weeks. Or, like Heather, you may find it an addiction. Regardless, there is a 76 percent chance that all this monitoring will not make your baby sleep through the night any sooner, but we can't stop you from graphing it just the same.

#14 *Make a time capsule.*

While you're hanging around your house in a postpartum haze, why not commemorate the era in which your baby was born by assembling a time capsule?

.... **THE OLD-FASHIONED WAY** ....

1 Decorate a file box with your baby's name.

2 Put the front section of the newspaper from her birthday inside.

3 Cut out pictures from magazines or catalogs that represent today's fashion.

4 Print a picture of your family car (a photo from a Web site is easiest).

5 Include a piece of technology with a note explaining what it does. A DVD, cell phone, or Palm Pilot represent the decade well.

.... **THE LAZY-WOMAN'S WAY** ....

1 Buy a disposable camera.

2 Take pictures of the stuff around your home and in your life.

3 Label the camera with the baby's name, birth date, and "Photo Time Capsule: Develop me in a few years."

4 Throw it in a keepsake box and let time pass.

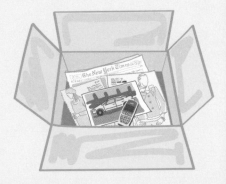

#15 *Find a cozy spot for a monthly picture.*

Find a good spot in your home to take the same picture each month. Use a comfy rocking chair or a certain place on the couch and photograph baby each month on her birthday.

When you look back over the 12 photos from this first year, you'll really see the baby grow before your eyes. For the first few months, the challenge will be to find a decent place where the baby won't tip over or get smooshed. As she grows, the new challenge will be to snap the picture before she climbs away or dials the phone. Ahhh, progress is a beautiful thing!

.... **PLACEMENT OPTIONS** ....

★ Lay your baby on a solid-colored sheet on your bed.

★ Snap a picture next to the same stuffed animal each month to show scale.

★ Position baby snuggly in a corner of the couch, with good lighting.

#16 *Go on a reconnaissance mission.*

When the baby is in a good mood (or better, sleeping peacefully in the stroller), scope out your local shopping destinations for "safe places" where you can feed and change her. That way you can get out of the house every day and know that you don't have to race against the clock to get back home. We recommend the children's area of any bookstore. Find a quiet corner and a tiny chair and pull out your boob or bottle.

If you aren't ready for public feeding this first month, we totally understand. Look around, make a mental note of where you see moms feeding babies, and come back next month to try it yourself. By the end of month 2, you'll probably have your own favorite places. Then you can accost other new mothers on the street and tell them where to go.

············ **ROOKIE MOM – RECOMMENDED SAFE FEEDING PLACES** ············

★ **Nordstrom women's lounges.** These have areas that are specially intended for feeding and changing—plus lots of nice old ladies who can watch your stuff or even your baby while you use the bathroom.

★ **Baby boutiques.** You'll usually find changing tables and chairs for feeding.

★ **Family restaurant chains.** They might be less crowded on weekdays, so you can get a big booth where all your stuff will fit. Rookie mom Sunny spent a large part of her maternity leave with baby Lucas in her local California Pizza Kitchen.

#17 *Pretend you're in Paris.*

This outing is perfect for beginners. Gather your baby and go to your favorite outdoor breakfast venue. Pack a journal, a trashy magazine, or a pile of thank-you notes and head to a café. Park the stroller right next to you and breathe in the fresh air. Before you leave, buy some baked treats for dessert tonight. *C'est magnifique!*

If it's raining, this outing is even better. You need to get out of the house, and your new favorite coffee shop is a place you can sit for an hour or two and just be proud that you went somewhere on your own. Yes, you can take the baby out in the rain or snow. Your mother surely took you. Go on! That hot chocolate has your name written all over it.

At this point in your baby's development, you have about 5 more months to enjoy café culture. And for your sake, we hope some of this time falls in the warmer months! Once your baby crawls, she won't be so tolerant of your fondness for people watching or spacing out, so live it up now.

#18 *Take picture of sleeping baby*

Sometimes young babies make annoyingly weird faces at the very same moment you're trying to take a picture that will prove their infinite cuteness to the world at large. If you're experiencing this dilemma, we suggest you snap a couple photos while your angel is asleep. A sleeping baby won't cry or cross her eyes or make a rooting face — she'll be peaceful and pleasant and cute as can be.

To show the rest of the world just how precious your new arrival is, cover the floor in a well-lit corner of your house with a solid-colored piece of fabric, such as a sheet, blanket, or pillowcase. Lay your unswaddled infant on the fabric, stand above so that you're looking down, and shoot the picture!

#19 Cut up your bra or mix it up!

Breastfeeding mamas: Take an old tank top or soft-cup bra and cut holes where your nipples go. Seriously. Sleep in this, or wear it whenever your nipples need to be untouched. (Though preferably not when your father-in-law is around.)

Formula-feeding mamas: Get the big kid-sized bottles and mix up 10 ounces before your own bedtime. Store it in the refrigerator. Now you won't have to do any measuring and mixing in the middle of the night—just pour from the big bottle into your little newborn bottle and run it under hot water.

#20 Get to first base and stay there.

This is the safest of sex. Keep all your clothes on, lie down, and make out with your partner. Let a few minutes of cuddling and kissing remind you both what romance feels like.

Intimacy may not be as spontaneous as it once was. It's perfectly okay to schedule it, discuss it, and limit it to whatever you're ready for. Keep it PG-rated for today. Try for another base next month.

Month

2

#21 *Keep in touch.*

Make a list of your friends and take it out whenever you are feeling lonely or isolated. In fact, you may already have a list of your friends, perhaps from your wedding or holiday card list. Call one of them each day, just to say hi.

Remember, your peeps may be afraid to contact you right now because they assume you're too busy. It's on you to reach out and let them know how you're doing. You'll have to work a little harder to keep up these relationships from now on, but it's work that's well worth doing. Go call someone from your list right now!

#22 *Go to the theater where crying is allowed.*

We thank God for TiVo, but also for movie theaters that have special showings for new parents. With clever names like "Mommy Matinee" or "Baby Brigade," these showings welcome babes in arms. Both of our babies were frequent attendees of baby movies during their first year. Find one in your area and make it a weekly habit. Don't worry; yours will (most likely) not be the loudest baby in the theater.

If your area doesn't have such a showing, try sneaking your baby into a weekday matinee with a friend. It's not officially encouraged by the theaters, but it works most of the time. You didn't hear it from us, but we confess to having done that, too.

#23 Master some one-handed tasks.

We've all heard that moms have eyes in the backs of their heads and can juggle 17 tasks at once. One day you will drive a carpool while quizzing spelling words, applying lipstick, and planning someone's birthday party in your head. But for now, let's keep it simple.

What kinds of things can you do while one hand is occupied with baby care (e.g., shoving in a pacifier, nursing, soothing, bottle feeding)? Why, lots of things! Do some prep work before getting busy with baby and you can:

1 **Eat a snack or mini meal.** Have cut or handheld food (sandwich, cold pizza) near your nursing station. Throw a dishtowel over the baby's head. Nothing dangerous, please.

2 **Write thank-you notes.** Have a stack of notes at the ready; write with your dominant hand and pacify with the weaker one.

3 **Type very slowly.** A well-positioned laptop or keyboard goes a long way toward this endeavor.

4 **Drink a frosty beverage.** Use a straw or a narrow-necked bottle.

5 **Read a book or magazine.** If you can keep it open with one hand, you can read it.

#24 Join a new mom's group.

We cannot emphasize enough the importance of hanging out with other women who are doing what you're doing. Swaddling, nursing, trying out bottles, using swings — these are some of the things you'll discuss. But there are also the sensitive issues of body image, careers, and relationships. It's quite likely that you and your partner are experiencing parenting a little differently. Finding other women with whom you can share your experiences is vital.

Furthermore, a mom's group is an excellent motivator for getting you out of the house. Group outings can give structure to your week: You make a commitment to go for a walk on Tuesday morning at 10 a.m., and by gosh, you better be there, no matter how many times you have to change your shirt before leaving the house.

We know that at this point, any other woman you see walking around with a stroller looks like a "real mother," but believe us, everyone is learning and struggling on the job. Being a new mom is like being a freshman in college. The people who live on your floor are likely to become your best friends, even if you had little in common to begin with. Find some strangers whose babies were born in the same month as yours and turn them into friends, or at least companions. Tell your birth stories with all the gory details, and you'll have nothing left to hide from these people.

To find a mom's group near you, talk to a childbirth educator, a lactation consultant, a prenatal yoga class instructor, or the programming facilitator at a church or synagogue. Or, start your own group by putting yourself out there on Craig's List or another neighborhood forum.

.... **LEADING YOUR OWN NEW MOM'S GROUP** ....

Our mom's groups had facilitators to guide discussions. If your group does not, here is our simple format suggestion:

★ **Meet twice a week.** One day can focus on talking and may take place at someone's house or a picnic area. The other day should be an outing that group members take turns organizing.
★ **Give everyone the chance to talk.** At the beginning of the discussion, circle up and allow each person to share one "high" and one "low" for the week.
★ **Create an e-mail list** to encourage discussion throughout the week.
★ **Vary the outings.** Use this book to inspire you to try new things together.

#25 Carry out more; wash dishes less.

Take a walk through the neighborhood and grab takeout or delivery menus from places you like, or, if you don't live within walking distance of any restaurants, drive around and pick up the menus. Try to keep 5 or 10 on hand for times when the idea of cooking is just too horrific.

To make your takeout nights even more convenient, program the phone numbers of your favorite places into your cell phone. Call and place an order just before your partner leaves work, and have him stop and pick up dinner on the way home. We've heard from more than a few dads that such an errand is a nice break between work and home, so everybody wins.

#26 Paint baby's feet.

Many paint-your-own-pottery places know how to help you get cute baby footprints on plates, mugs, picture frames, and the like. Flat tile was the cheapest thing to paint, so we made trivets, those things you put underneath hot dishes so they don't mark your table.

Paint everything you want on your piece while baby sleeps (or a friend holds him), then do the feet and race out the door because he's likely to be cranky when he wakes up. At least that's how it was for us.

#27 *Encourage daddy time, and relax already!*

Mama, your partner needs your support (but not your controlling or bossing) to become a confident and competent parent.

Let him take the lead in diaper changes, baby bathing, and shushing while you go in the other room and put your feet up. Encourage dad and baby to develop a routine of regular evening walks together. Try your very best not to micromanage or give "helpful hints." For some rookie moms, it's easiest to leave the house completely to avoid watching or listening to the two of them together. The happy byproduct is that you can take a break! Like it or not, they will be perfectly fine without you.

#28 *Drink beer.*

If you're nursing, beer is widely rumored to help with milk production. If you aren't nursing, beer might still help you deal with the crying (yours and baby's). Also, it's worth mentioning that we're talking about one beer a day, not a whole case. . .

#29 *Think with your melons; after all, some men think with. . . .*

This next bit probably falls into the very large bucket of "nobody ever told me this was going to happen": If you're a nursing mom, your breasts might get all tingly sometimes for no apparent reason. This phenomenon may be triggered by hearing another baby cry; having any emotion at all (sadness, confusion, joy, whatever); seeing the words "hot chocolate" on a menu.

If you have this feeling in the first months of your baby's life, use your special superpower to make decisions. When you start to get a funny feeling in your chest as you read a menu, you are probably biologically programmed to *need* that very food. Order the hot chocolate (or whatever your boobs want) and enjoy!

Appreciate this phenomenon while it lasts. Before you know it, it will pass, and you'll just be a regular person with regular boobies once again.

#30 *Have some adult conversation.*

Come up with one "outside" topic to discuss with your partner over dinner, and challenge him to do the same. Or, if you really want to put yourself to the test, find three topics to bring up tonight. Your subject can be anything from world news to neighborhood gossip, but it cannot be about the contents of diapers.

When Heather and her husband were preparing to hang out with friends for an entire weekend, they each came up with five separate non-baby-related topics of discussion to uphold their reputation as an interesting couple. Try to remember that when people want to know how life with baby is, even your real friends want a short response, not a detailed description of your baby's sleeping schedule.

#31 *Come home to a clean house.*

Treat yourself to a cleaning person. If this is not something your family can afford regularly, splurge a little, once, as a special gift. Take baby out for some fun and come home to spotless floors and a made bed.

Enjoy it, and maybe photograph it, 'cause it ain't gonna last.

#32 *Figure out birth control.*

We're not going to lie to you: If you have sex, you may get pregnant. It doesn't matter if you have a 6-week-old, are nursing round-the-clock, and required fertility treatment to get pregnant the first time. Your inner workings could be secretly recovered before you know it.

If you think about it for a moment, you can probably come up with a pair of siblings who are just about 1 year apart. If this is how you want to grow your family, pick a method of birth control and start using it.

#33 *Reinvent a burp cloth.*

Plain white burp cloths are no fun to barf on, Mom! Give your baby a target to aim for by decorating a few cloth diapers with your handiwork.

1 **Purchase (or borrow) plastic stencils and nontoxic fabric paint.** You can find loads of options at a craft supply store.
2 **Slide a piece of waxed paper underneath a boring cloth diaper.**
3 **Place a stencil on top of the diaper.**
4 **With a paintbrush or sponge brush, dab paint inside stencil.**
5 **Remove the stencil.** Voilà! Your burp cloth is boring no more.

#34 Rub your baby down with infant massage.

Sign up for a baby massage class at a yoga studio to learn the basics. As long as you start slowly and watch the baby for cues, massage can be fun for both of you, even if you're making it up as you go. Try to relax and enjoy the moment as you get to know your baby's developing body. You can build up to a longer massage when you're both ready, but even a short one is like a mini workout, leaving babies happy, hungry for dinner, and ready for bed.

.... **SOME QUICK TIPS AND IDEAS** ....

* **Keep the room warm and cozy.** Throw some hand towels in the dryer beforehand (one for underneath and one to cover the baby while you're working on other bits).
* **Use a little bit of olive oil on your hands.**
* **Talk through what you're doing.** (Say, "I'm using my thumbs to make swirly motions on your teeny tiny foot.")
* **Let dad try it.** Don't supervise.
* **Try a massage while traveling.** You'll help baby unwind and feel "at home."
* **Move on if your little buddha seems annoyed.** Try another body part, or give it up entirely.

#35 *Introduce your stroller to the mall and buy some new jeans.*

Put away the maternity pants and take yourself out to get some interim jeans that make you feel normal. Go with a girlfriend you trust. Don't look at the size; just find something flattering and comfortable.

DO NOT THINK ABOUT OR TALK ABOUT THE WEIGHT YOU ARE GOING TO LOSE IN THE FUTURE. Buy jeans to wear this week. When the day comes, you can put these jeans in storage for the next time around, give them to a friend who is a few months behind you, or wear them when you paint that mural you've been talking about.

#36 *Write a baby-sized shopping list.*

If you haven't gone to the grocery store yet, make your first trip a practice run. Use a shopping cart, but just buy a treat for yourself. That way, when you actually have to go grocery shopping, you'll know you can do it. There are two ways to approach the cart:

1 **Wear your baby in a front carrier or sling** and push the cart.
2 **Put the entire infant car seat in the cart.** Make sure it doesn't wobble.

Don't try to be a hero and carry your baby in your arms while also picking up the groceries. The shopping cart is your friend.

#37 *Snap a photo of your family's feet.*

Play Twister! Pick the room in your house that gets the most natural sunlight and open the blinds to let it in. (For best results, turn off the flash.) Lay down a solid-colored sheet or blanket. Have fun as a family of three figuring out what position will best allow you to capture everyone's feet at once — sitting, standing, or lying down. What a great excuse to get a pedicure!

#38 *Bounce it out.*

Our mothers might swear by clothes dryers and vacuum cleaners, but we've found that a yoga ball is a great tool for soothing a crying baby. Sit on it, holding the swaddled baby, and bounce to a consistent rhythm.

If you don't have a yoga ball, sit on the edge of your bed and bounce while you hold the baby. If someone is visiting and wants to help soothe the baby, show her this trick and then go take a hot shower so you don't eavesdrop.

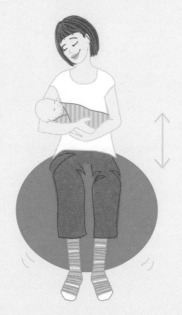

#39 *Announce baby's arrival.*

If you haven't gotten around to it yet, it's time to find a cute picture of Junior and send out your baby announcements. Crafty ladies can make their own announcements on the computer and print them on card stock. One of the big photo Web sites can make this task even easier.

To make your announcement more memorable (or gift-worthy!) add some creative details. You may have thought you would never become such a cheeseball, but childbirth does strange things to our sensibilities.

.... **GET SILLY WITH YOUR BIG NEWS** ....

★ Add a funny quote, like, Aunt Sharon says, "Cutest baby ever!"

★ Use a rock-and-roll theme and list the vital stats in the manner of concert tour dates.

★ Select a unique border and compose a headline to match. (E.g., "Our little cowgirl has arrived" with a lasso motif.)

#40 Bond with family.

These people are your best chance at free childcare. If your relatives are not total nutjobs, ask them to come hold the baby so you can do something else for a while (the over-50 crowd tends to be pretty psyched to have this job). If your relatives *are* total nutjobs, can you think of a friend's family who would like to see more of your cute baby?

Take lots of pictures of each family member holding the baby because you'll get in trouble if you forget!

#41 Go bowling.

Some nights we think there should be a white noise soundtrack with sounds like "bowling alley" to lull babies to sleep.

If your baby is noisy or lulled to sleep by loud noises, meet some pals for bowling one afternoon. This is a fun activity for a mom's group or for a double or triple date with those friends you haven't seen for the past 3 months.

Even a rookie mom knows: Bring some hand sanitizer, and don't forget to wear socks.

#42 Curl up and dye.

If you're dragging your sorry new mama butt around looking as haggard as you feel, we think its time to clean up your act.

Here are some pick-me-up suggestions that will give you a few moments of pampering, followed by a month or so of compliments:

1 **Get a nice haircut.** The hair washing alone is worth the outing.
2 **Clean up your brows.** Dark-haired lovelies, have a pro give you a new expression with wax and a tweeze.
3 **Tint your lashes.** Fair-haired beauties, putting a fake coat of mascara on your lashes will make you look awake in all the inevitable new-baby photos. This is far more efficient than daily makeup application, and it allows the truly lazy among us to look somewhat put together with little effort.

Then just apply some tinted lip balm and you're ready to leave the house to collect your compliments ("Have you lost weight?" and "Motherhood really agrees with you").

#43 Go on a little date with your mate.

If lounging around the house in your jammies every evening is starting to lose its allure, snap out of it. For the first few months of your baby's life, he really is quite portable. (Maybe not so portable as he was when you were pregnant, but have you seen those families with toddlers?!)

Pack up the bucket seat or baby wrap and bring him along for a short date with your mate: a simple dinner out, a long walk together, or even just a piece of pie à la mode.

#44 Photograph a nasty crying jag.

Snap a picture of a crying fit. Or two. Or one each month. You have lots of pictures of baby being cute, so take a few that will remind you how hard this first year really is. You may feel a little mean doing it—but it will only take a second. If you're really heartless, take some video.

Do this now, because when your baby is a bouncing 8-month-old who doesn't cry very much, you will lose perspective and begin to believe that your baby has always been a joy to be around. You might even think that having another baby is a good idea. Pictures and video of inconsolable crying will keep you grounded.

Month

3

#45 Practice yoga, baby style.

Many yoga studios offer mom-and-baby classes. Search online for "postnatal yoga" and the name of your city to find one.

Benefits of these classes include getting out of the house, being kind to your body, meeting other rookie moms, and sometimes learning a little baby massage technique.

Some classes have "helpers" who will hold a baby needing some cuddling while mommy stretches. Our favorite pose is the one in which you just lie on the floor and do nothing. It is definitely worth paying for.

#46 Count your steps.

We both enjoy tracking things, and counting steps has become an on-and-off obsession for us. It's fun! Invest in a pedometer and aim for 10,000 steps each day. You'll be surprised how many steps a mom can take just running around the house, but to reach 10,000, you'll need to take a walk outside for sure. This is good motivation to get some fresh air.

One day toward the end of her maternity leave, the ever-competitive Heather set her personal best of 17,236 steps. Can you beat that?

#47 Brainstorm the things you like to do.

We challenge you to make a list of 50 things you like to do. This sounds like a self-help suggestion, but it's actually really fun. When you've finished your list, look it over to see how many of these incorporate your new role as a mom and which ones require you to find some childcare.

Hang on to this valuable resource and refer to it on your birthday or days off from regular responsibilities. See how many of your favorite things can be packed into one day.

The best part of this activity is trading your list with your friends and/or spouse if you convince them to do it, too.

.... **AN EXCERPT FROM WHITNEY'S LIST** ....

34 Have slumber parties at Tahoe cabins

35 Be complimented for my creative ideas at work

36 Check the mail

37 Cross-country ski when it's sunny

38 Eat fish tacos and have piña coladas on Friday night

39 Fall asleep on the couch

40 Give handmade gifts

#48 *Interrupt someone's workday.*

Visiting your partner at work is something to look forward to for all involved. It's probably feasible in some form for most professions. (If your partner works at home or does not work, go visit a friend or your old coworkers.)

You may assume you'll do this all the time while on maternity leave, but it turned out to be a rare occasion for us. Therefore, we now see it as a major outing.

We also figured that we'd be spending time *in* the office, showing off the baby to coworkers. But when we visited our spouses, they were more interested in getting out of the office to see their little families than in taking the baby around to colleagues. No problem there. Who needs all those germy people putting their hands on baby, anyway?

One last exciting development was getting to use a restroom alone. What a special event! Make sure you take advantage of it.

#49 *Treat yourself to a pedicure.*

While baby is still small enough for the infant carrier, take advantage of your relative "freedom" to get your toenails done. Once baby begins toddling, a pedicure will be truly impossible.

You might be lucky enough to live near a spa that offers special services to mommies (like access to a baby swing). If not, here are a few ways to make do:

* ★ Place baby in the car seat on a chair next to you.
* ★ Hold baby in your arms during the treatment.
* ★ Wear baby in a sling.
* ★ Bring a friend, sibling, or parent along and ask them to walk baby around the block in the stroller while you enjoy yourself.

#50 *Let her be.*

Do not to try to make a happy baby happier. Deep thought, eh? A person blissfully staring into space does not need her mother to shake a rattle in her face.

Don't be afraid to give baby some alone time in the crib. Do you need to do some online research, uninterrupted? Need to put away groceries or talk to a friend? Put some music on in baby's room, or turn on her mobile, and let her be for a while.

#51 Engineer a food train.

One rookie mom we know, Jeanine, gets dinner delivered to her house three Thursdays a month. On the fourth Thursday, it's her turn—she "drives the dinner train" and takes a meal to three of her friends.

Find a friend or three with whom you can exchange meals on a regular basis to spice up your culinary life. More important, this activity provides you with the opportunity to take a few nights off from cooking while still getting a home-cooked dinner on the table. All aboard!

#52 Go retro at a drive-in movie.

Gosh, do they still have these where you live? A drive-in movie is a great event for a bucket-seat baby. You and your mate can pretend to be wild teenagers (or really shy teenagers) in the front seat.

Split a soda pop and some popcorn or bring your own favorite foods. Remember to cheer for the cartoon hotdog as he jumps into the bun.

#53 Build muscles at boot camp.

By the time Julian was 10 weeks old, Whitney had not exercised for about 6 months. Baby Bootcamp was her official reintroduction to sweating, and she loved it. These stroller-friendly classes are offered in most cities and suburbs—search the Web for exercise classes that include baby. Led by an instructor, you'll push your stroller around a course, stopping every few minutes to do conditioning exercises. Give it a try—you're likely to find these classes manageable even if you're not a gym-goer in normal life.

············· **HERE'S WHY** ·············

1 **Exercising in the company of other sleep-deprived, temporarily overweight, leaky-breasted women is more fun.**

2 **Stepping away from the class to deal with a fussy baby is par for the course.**

3 **It nudges you out of the house** to do something good for your body and to enjoy the outdoors.

4 **It's no problem to walk the course rather than run it.** (Whitney had many excuses lined up for not running, some of which are valid, and most of which are shared by other participants.)

Once you have the hang of it, invite your partner and show off your awesome athleticism.

#54 *Take a break.*

Schedule a mental break for at least a half hour each day. Every day. Zoning out in front of the TV or Internet does not really count toward reclaiming your sanity. The world will still turn if you are not hands-on with your baby every second, and you might as well get used to the idea now.

············ **HERE ARE SOME SIMPLE IDEAS FOR CHILLING** ············

★ **A cup of tea and your journal ★ A trashy magazine and a snack ★**
★ **A phone call with a good friend ★**

#55 *Write your birth story.*

Before you forget it completely, write out your labor and delivery experience in as much detail as you can remember.

Was your daughter a 4-hour labor capped off with a piece of chocolate cake or a 44-hour delivery with nothing but ice chips? Inquiring minds will want to know.

Lord it over your kid as needed later in life.

#56 *Talk about sex.*

You heard us, woman.

If it's not happening yet, let's assume you are terrified, disinterested, or terrified by your disinterest. Talk to your other mom friends about it. You are not the first person in history who wasn't ready to get back in the game after the doctor-prescribed post-birth 6-week waiting period.

Talking about it will help you feel normal. It's hard to break the ice on this conversation, so you might try a subtle introduction: "Hey [*lifelong friend's name who has a child one year older than yours*], it's [*your name*]. I'm calling to talk about sex. Do you have time right now?"

If you feel abnormal after talking to your friends, talk to your doctor. She's heard it all before, and she might have some suggestions.

The most important person to talk to, however, is your partner. Take things one "base" at a time, like a high school couple.

#57 Stay tuned in.

Are your parents "out of it"? Do they know who Gwen Stefani is? Be warned: Now that you're a parent, this could happen to you.

Don't get stuck listening to Dave Matthews for the rest of your life. Soon he will be comparable to Neil Diamond. Turn on the radio. If something sounds good to you, follow up. Download some songs or buy the CD.

#58 Eat your way around the world.

Liven up your existence by exploring new cuisines and cultures through the miracle of take-out. Expand the theme you've selected with a quick visit to the iTunes store (or eMusic or Netflix) so you can set the mood and make the meal feel special, even though it's coming out of plastic cartons.

And, um, rookies, don't hurt yourself with costumes and decorations. The important thing is to find an easy way out of your culinary rut, not to sew matching lederhosen for the family.

············ **SOME ETHNIC CUISINES TO EXPLORE** ············

★ Korean ★ Moroccan ★ Ethiopian ★ Mexican ★ Jamaican ★ Japanese ★
★ Italian ★ Hungarian ★ Thai ★ Greek ★ Afghani ★

#59 *Take a walk on the wild side.*

Yep, we're still trying to get you out of the house. Make your walk a little longer and leave your comfort zone today by checking out a different part of town. Even light industrial areas have noises and sights that might appeal to babies (just beware toxic smells and enormous trucks!).

Take your camera and shoot some photos of the stroller in front of the most un-babyish sites you come across. Examples include adult entertainment venues, liquor stores, and tattoo parlors.

#60 *Design your own baby clothes.*

We often admire the expensive-but-clever baby bodysuits with ironic sayings across the chest. You certainly have some of your own brilliant ideas for T-shirt-worthy slogans: Funny nicknames, favorite pictures, and family jokes are better than anything you can find in a trendy children's boutique.

Make personalized baby clothes on the cheap, using your computer and special iron-on transfer paper that works with most home printers. Paste an image into Microsoft Word or make word art in Powerpoint, then print the image on the magical iron-on paper, available at office supply stores. Use multipacks of bodysuits as your canvas.

#61 *Shop with your little buddy.*

You can do it. Visit a shopping district you enjoyed before acquiring your new sidekick. Strap the baby onto your front to keep your profile slim and to free your hands for caressing the merchandise.

You may want to bring a stroller to tote along your new purchases. It's also a good spot to stow the baby if you simply must try something on.

#62 Go for a swim.

Taking the baby to a swimming pool is both scary and funny.

If you're alone, carefully think through the logistics of how you will change your clothes, change the baby, enter the pool, get out of the pool, put on dry clothes, and return to the car.

The first time you try it, you'll probably mess up part of the process and end up walking out to your car in just a bra and towel, holding your baby in one arm and a diaper between your teeth. Let us help you out: Take your stroller with you into the dressing room. That way you have someplace to put the baby, towels, wet bathing suits, and diaper bag while you dry yourself.

Check your local public pools or gym to see when "family swim time" is scheduled. Usually these pools are heated for the comfort of babies and senior citizens. It's nice for us mamas, too.

#63 *Bake cookies one at a time.*

One side effect of raging hormones is that when you want something, you want it now! Here are two ways to have piping-hot cookies about 20 minutes after the mood strikes you.

············ Option 1: **HOMEMADE** ············

1 When the baby is sleeping, mix up a batch of your favorite cookie dough.

2 Bake yourself two cookies as a reward for your trouble. Form the rest into little balls on a cookie sheet (as close together as you can get 'em).

3 Put the cookie sheet with the little cookie dough wads in the freezer.

4 In the morning, put the frozen cookie dough wads into a large freezer bag labeled with the correct baking temp and time. Add about 2 minutes to the normal baking time to compensate for the frozen state of your cookie dough.

············ Option 2: **STORE-BOUGHT** ············

1 Pay a visit to the refrigerator or freezer section in your local market.

2 Pick up a tube (or box or whatever) of prepared cookie dough.

3 Turn on the oven, scoop out a couple cookies, bake, and you're done.

Some gourmet bakeries also offer prepared cookie dough, so if you're feeling fancy, make some phone calls for a gastronomic adventure.

#64 Force baby to model new outfits.

When you're home alone with baby and no one is watching, pull out all the new outfits you got as gifts, no matter how silly you think they are*, and photograph her in the clothes before she outgrows them.

Remember to take pictures when each outfit is fresh. This is especially important if your baby is a spontaneous puker.

Think of this as "playing baby doll." After all, why did we have children if not to pretend they're our favorite toys?

* For truly ugly outfits, once the modeling session is over, you can sell them (see #186 on page 159) or party with 'em (see #68 on page 65).

#65 Sing, sing a song.

Sometimes we want to remind our babies that we are still there even though they can't see us from their position in the car seat or bouncy seat. Let loose and start singing—any genre will do. Your musical voice will reassure your babe that you haven't left the room.

Surely there's at least one song for which you know all the words. If you must, refresh your memory by looking up the lyrics online so you can belt them out with confidence as you drive or shower.

Rolling Over and Rolling With It

MONTHS 4 THROUGH 6

Once your baby smiles and laughs, the occasions when you want the stork to come back and pick him up are fewer and farther between, aren't they? Get ready to have a bit more fun and try some new things. Your baby is doing the same.

.... YOUR NEW SKILLS ....

* ★ Carrying a baby in one hand and a diaper bag, camera, and keys in another
* ★ Having a slight clue about when your baby needs to go to sleep
* ★ Calling your friends and talking about something other than your baby
* ★ Changing a diaper in public

.... YOUR NEW FEARS ....

* ★ You should or shouldn't go back to work
* ★ Your hair is going to keep falling out until you are entirely bald
* ★ Your old pants will never fit again
* ★ You'll mess up baby's nap schedule if you do something fun for yourself

Since you're gaining confidence, and worrying less that you might break your baby, you can socialize more and plan fun outings. There are plenty of things to do at home while baby naps or in the evenings with your partner when baby's in bed for the night. And if you find yourself totally bored (we know, we know, the baby still doesn't make any of his own plans or ask you how your day is going), we have photography assignments you can take on. Try to ditch your anxiety and just roll with it.

Month

4

#66 *Enjoy modern art.*

Assume you go to a cocktail party sometime soon. When someone asks what you do, instead of mumbling about maternity leave or bursting into tears when you think about how you can't drink much because you have to nurse every 3 hours and wake up at 6 A.M., change the subject and say "Have you seen the Rothko show?"

Facilitate this conversation by packing yourself up and heading into the city for a museum outing. Take time for a nice lunch at the museum's café and practice what you're going to say at that cocktail party.

#67 *Shower at the gym.*

Katie, a rookie mom in Berkeley, California, said that when her baby was 3 months old she started using the gym as her primary shower location.

Leave the baby in childcare and go take a long one. Blow dry and apply makeup if that makes you happy. Don't worry, if you don't work out first, we won't tell anyone.

#68 *Host an ugly baby (clothes) contest.*

People who don't have babies think that everything that fits the under-12-pound set is adorable, just because it's so tiny. But for those of us who are living in this phase, clothes for 3- to 6-month-olds look perfectly normal — and this is when you start getting picky. You realize all small things are not cute. Some are just plain awful! What was that gift-giver thinking? Does she hate your baby? Does she think yellow ducklings are a good motif for a boy who can practically put his own binky in his mouth?

Host a costume party and ugly-clothing contest. Invite some other babies to come over wearing their worst attire and dress your baby in his ugliest outfit. Dorky gifts, ratty hand-me-downs, and hopeless mismatches will finally have their day.

Try not to be offended if your idea of the cutest outfit ever winds up on one of the other models. Cute is completely in the eye of the beholder.

Take lots of pictures, but be careful who sees them!

#69 *Sleep late.*

Frankly, late might be a stretch for some of us. But you can sleep *later* with your partner's help. Trade off to get some extra Zzzzzz's on the weekend. You deserve it.

To truly make this work, your partner should get up with the baby and take care of the first feeding out of earshot of the bedroom. Then they should leave the house so that the sounds of your baby crying, cooing, or grunting in the other room don't keep you from sleeping. Because really, sitting on the couch and reading *Pat the Bunny* twice before coming in to see if you're ready to play does not count as giving you a break.

#70 *Count your mommy friends.*

Make a list of your mom friends so you can work your network when you have a weird question about sleeping, wonky nipples, babysitters, playgrounds—anything! It can be a written list you post someplace in case you want to do a quick survey or an e-mail "group" you set up in your e-mail program.

#71 Accessorize!

Feeling flabby, dull, or not quite yourself? Maybe your clothes still don't fit properly?

Forget about the problem areas and focus on a solution: Draw attention away from your "muffin top" and punch up your appearance with stylish accessories.

Carry a modern bag or wear dramatic earrings. Think new scarf, cute hair clip, loud socks, sassy hat. Before you head out the door for an outing with your adorable but drool-covered sidekick, put on something that will make you smile.

#72 Read a book for YOU.

Pick up a non-parenting book to fill your brain with something other than poop and sleep. If you're using a breast pump, you have a unique opportunity to get some reading done. If you're a limber breastfeeder, try holding the book with your "extra" hand. And if you're a regular mommy narcoleptic, reading a few pages (or sentences) might be nice before your bedtime.

#73 *"Heart" someone or something.*

Putting cute messages across your baby's chest is all the rage. Whether you're a "Daddy's Little Princess" type or an "I'm smarter than the President" type, try your hand at making your own, using the classic template from "I ♥ NY" shirts and shopping bags.

A straightforward message to Daddy or Mommy will do, as in "I ♥ Daddy." But we prefer a more subtle personalization, with a reference to our own interests, such as "I ♥ downloading music for free" or "I ♥ burritos."

.... **THREE WAYS TO GET YOUR MESSAGE ACROSS** ....

1 Make the design on a computer, printed on iron-on transfer paper (available in office-supply stores).

2 Use two Sharpies—black and red—and your free hand. (Looks better than you think!)

3 Buy iron-on lettering at a craft store.

#74 *Arrange for the groceries to come to you.*

Grocery store trips are easier when all you need is a few things (and you can escape before anyone melts down). Keep your store trips manageable by using an online grocery delivery service to stock up on heavy and nonperishable items at once. In addition to saving you the trouble of lugging all those bags, online grocers also allow you to keep a running shopping list, so that you don't have to figure out what to buy every time. Check around to see which stores offer the service in your area.

If you're picky about your fruits and vegetables, do an online search for "organic delivery" and your city's name; there may be services in your area that specialize in fresh, organic produce.

#75 *Knit with your baby.*

There is a lovely knitting shop near us that invites us to come and knit with other moms, babies, and moms-to-be.

If you don't know how to knit, know that most yarn shops have classes and often offer one-on-one instruction. We've heard of at least one expectant mom's club at a knitting store, and a few others told us that "babies are always welcome."

.... **OTHER REASONS TO GET OUT THE KNITTING NEEDLES** ....

★ **Motivates you to sort through your scary bag of yarn;** or, if you aren't the type who has yarn in your house, motivates you to go to a yarn store to buy some

★ **Gives you something to do while your partner is watching boring TV** or hogging the computer

★ **Fosters a greater appreciation of the three naps a day your baby may be taking**

#76 Make your own list of boredom busters.

We aren't at all offended if some of the activities in this book don't appeal to you. We are, however, a little disappointed if you read the whole book and still can't think of anything to do today.

Next step: Take out a sheet of paper and write down 20 or so of the activities in this book you think you'd actually do (without swearing at us or crying). Add some of your own ideas.

Cut your activities into strips and put them in a jar, empty tissue box, or your underwear drawer. When boredom strikes, pull out an activity and get on it. Remember, it doesn't work if you just read the activity and *think* it sounds fun. You actually have to pack your diaper bag and take action.

#77 Visit a fabric store.

Take a walk through a fabric store with your baby in a front carrier. Let him touch all the different fabrics, faux furs, zippers, and doodads, under close supervision.

If you're game, pick up some bright buttons to sew onto your most boring baby clothes to give them a little more pizzazz.

#78 Hold hands.

One advantage of the hands-free baby carrier over a stroller is that either you or your partner can wear it while simultaneously doing something romantic with your hands. Grab your partner's hand (or butt) while walking merrily down the street. Skipping, however, is not recommended.

#79 Be fearless on Fridays.

We all have our own fears that prevent us from trying new things. You might be afraid to leave the house, to nurse in public, to commit to a social engagement, or to wear anything that makes you look fat.

We challenge you to confront your fears once a week this month (or, heck, all year!). Do something that scares you, whether it's taking your baby downtown, sneaking in a shower while she's in her crib, or changing a diaper in the trunk of your car.

Identify exactly what you fear. Is it that the baby will cry and you'll feel guilty? That you'll feel embarrassed? That people will think you're a bad mother? That you'll feel overwhelmed and disorganized? That the baby will be hurt? That you'll forget something you need? Once you've figured out what your real fear is, you can try to approach it with fearlessness.

#80 *Drive-through your baby's nap.*

If your baby likes to sleep in the car seat, consider patronizing nearby drive-through businesses so you can have a destination when you get in the car. Maybe it's an In-N-Out Burger or a drive-through Starbucks.

If you're brave and persuasive like Heather, you might even get other businesses to serve you curbside when it's slow. While you're out doing our environment a disservice by driving around to keep the baby asleep, call a local baby-goods store and ask if they can bring out a few necessities. They may even process your credit card right there at your car. Keep the phone number of a store like this in your cell phone. Seriously, Heather tried it, and it worked.

#81 *Chat about movies.*

If a book club is just too much of a time commitment, consider starting a movie club with other mom (or not mom) friends. In the span of a month, make sure you see the designated film and then meet at someone's house to share your lucid observations and eat dessert. Let your mate stay home, put the baby to bed, and play video games while you're gone.

#82 Sign up for lessons.

If any of your hobbies are languishing, now's the time to rev them back up again.

Find a weekly class (pottery, wine appreciation, public speaking, Italian) to get your creative juices flowing again. Committing to your own fun and enrichment can easily fall to the bottom of the to-do list, but paying for a class can bump it back to the top.

We know one rookie mom who took a painting class while her husband put the baby to bed during cry-it-out sleep training. Now, that's money well spent!

#83 Experiment at night.

It can take years of single living for a grown-up to perfect the ritual of "eat ice cream, brush teeth, fall asleep in bed while watching TV on the timer." Why would your baby be any different? Try introducing different variations on timing and combinations of bed, bath, book, bottle, singing, and goodnighting to everything in the house to see what works for you guys.

Consistency may be essential as baby gets older. But if you don't want to find yourself singing Christmas carols every night until your kid goes to college, play around now with a few variations on the nighttime theme. How is a new parent supposed to know what works without trial and error?

#84 Wear the baby.

Wearing your baby keeps him happy, especially if he's the type who likes to be held all the time. Once the baby is situated in the sling, you'll feel free as a bird. When he's strapped in, you can use your hands for other things, like dialing the phone, telling a story in which you gesture wildly for emphasis, or typing. Some women are able to nurse while wearing their baby in a sling. We bow to them.

If you're unsure of which sling or front carrier will work best for you, get together with some friends and swap some devices to see how you and baby like them.

#85 *Develop your photos further.*

By now your baby is actually cute, right? Consider getting note cards with baby's face on them; these are great for thank-you notes, invitations, or announcements, and you won't believe how thrilled the grandparents will be to get a set of their own.

Also, if you've been clogging the inboxes of your friends and family with billboard-sized photos, quit it already. Set up some online albums you can share. While you're shopping around for a photo Web site, you'll discover the many interesting ways to put your kid's mug on a mug. Your little dumpling can grace the side of just about anything these days. Have fun!

WHIMSICAL PHOTO PRODUCTS
.... WE CAN'T BELIEVE ARE OUT THERE ....

★ Deck of playing cards ★ Custom basketball hoop ★
★ License plate ★ Pillowcases ★ Candy tins ★

Month

5

#86 Share the spotlight.

Jump in the picture! Too often there are tons of pictures of baby with friends and family, but only a few with Mom and baby because we moms are usually behind the camera.

It's time to change that habit. Make friends with the auto-timer function on your camera. Take some shots of you and your little one. Be generous with the picture button. Go nuts. Even if the shots aren't your idea of perfection, you'll be glad you did it. It's a fun way to spend 20 minutes, and a great bonding activity.

Plus, you really need to think ahead. Twenty years from now, it's your hair and clothes (not to mention your car and furniture!) that'll be so dang funny. Give your child that gift.

#87 Play in another kind of nursery.

Take baby to a large outdoor plant store. Let her touch and listen to the wind chimes on display, play in the water fountain, tour the orchid hothouse, and watch the koi in the water-garden pond.

#88 *Talk about something other than sleep.*

Are your mama friends' discussions so dominated by the theme of sleep that you are starting to get sick of one another? We understand. But the fact is, you need each other *desperately* because no one else wants to hear you talk in such detail about your child's poorly timed wakefulness.

For the good of you all, e-mail the group and propose a moratorium on the subject of sleep at your next gathering. Suggest a list of alternative topics that will help rejuvenate you and make you laugh.

.... **HERE ARE SOME CONVERSATION STARTERS** ....

These may sound obvious, but when you've spent all your bonding time discussing naps and nipples, you probably left out some basic facts.

★ **What brought you to live here?**
★ **Where did you go to college and what did you study?**
★ **What were you going to name the baby if it was the opposite gender?**
★ **Tell us about the relationship you had before you were with your partner.**

#89 Swing out, sister.

If your little one's head control is solid, it's time to try a few minutes on the playground's baby swing. Watch baby very closely and maybe support his frame by filling in the space around him with blankets. This first swing moment is definitely a photo op.

Even if you're only up for a 5-minute visit, it's still worth seeking out your local park's baby swing location. You'll be spending lots of time here over the next couple years, so you might as well ease into it. At this point, a swing-outing may still be more fun for you than for baby; nothing prompts you to feel more like an official mom than going to the park with your child for the first time.

#90 *Write your own "momoirs."*

Although you might be recording some lovey-dovey stuff for your baby in a special book, you don't want to forget how you really felt, the mistakes you made, and the aspects of your experience as a mother that are unique to you.

You know enough now to write a few paragraphs about each month of your baby's life so far. Tuck it away in a private file, and try to keep it real. Don't let all your memories read back like a sappy greeting card.

#91 *Pimp your ride.*

When your kidlet makes the transition to the big-girl car seat, you'll soon learn that there is no sun visor. Instead of listening to the wailing of a sun-blinded baby or juggling those lame screens, arrange to have your rear windows tinted. It's not that expensive, and your baby will feel like a movie star.

Call a few places to compare prices. Some companies will even come to your house and install them right there in your driveway. This service is wonderful if you're jailed by a napping baby. If you're at work, schedule the service to come to your parking lot. Find out if your area has any legal restrictions on the degree of tint. You don't want to find out the hard way that you went too far.

#92 *Cover your assets.*

Parents in the professional world, or those who are about to have a hot date, should protect their clothing. Pick an old, large fleece pullover and designate it as your pre-work/date cover-up. Get dressed for work in your cashmere sweater set, dry-cleaned blazer, or whatever your uniform is, and then throw the fleece on overtop.

Do your last-minute baby snuggling (without worrying about spit up or snot on your shirt), head for the door, and remove the fleece on the way.

Sorry, we can't help you if the kid barfs on your trousers.

#93 *Turn OFF the TV.*

Step away from the remote control. After a hard day of dealing with a baby, the easiest thing to do is to zone out in front of the TV. We know. It's a bizarre form of nirvana to just flop there, watch some light, happy fare in short 22-minute increments, and plod off to bed.

But something remarkable will happen if you institute a no-TV-night ritual. You'll actually have time to talk, reconnect, play games, cook, plow through the family to-do list, and rest. Try it.

#94 *Write a status report.*

Now that you're parents, you may find that you need to check in more frequently with your partner. But whether you're at work or at home, you'll be more effective if you're not interrupting him with your every observation and question. Instead of calling your sweetie each time, try jotting some stuff down in a businesslike report. Prioritize what you share, and communication will be more pleasant.

STATE OF THE BABY

★ Extra whiny today. ★ Finally getting those teeth. ★ Tylenol before second nap. ★

Accomplishments

★ Test-drove strollers; I have two new favorites. ★
★ Bought two bibs. (Let's not lose these.) ★
★ Got new rice cereals to try. Here's hoping! ★
★ The sink overflowed when I left water running—oops! ★

Open Issues

★ Do you prefer red stroller or brown? I want to buy it today. ★
★ Babysitter for Saturday night. ★
★ Can you sit home with Milo next Monday? Book club? ★

Your Action Items

★ Fax the insurance claim. ★ Pick up mom's birthday present while downtown. ★

#95 *Put your family on a meal plan.*

Having trouble getting dinner on the table? Us, too! One solution is to plan meals in advance, when you have the time and brain space. Then you can more easily get food to the table. It goes something like this:

1 **Sunday night, think about the week in meals.** Review cookbooks and magazines, ask friends what they're eating, and/or check the cupboards, fridge, and freezer to see what you already have.

2 **Write down a week's worth of meals.** Don't kid yourself into thinking you're making a full set of recipes every night. Be realistic about how much you take out, go out, or eat leftovers and slot those into your week as well.

3 **The day of, make sure you have what you need.** Do this early in the day, when time isn't tight.

4 **Trade off with your partner.** Whichever parent is not actively feeding and putting baby to bed can make the dinner you've planned.

#96 *Personalize your thank-you notes.*

Show, don't tell, your favorite gift-givers how much you appreciate the goodies they've given you. Take a picture of your baby wearing the outfit, lying on the blanket, or playing with the toy.

Use a photo Web site to turn your image into a postcard and mail it; or just stick a copy of the picture into the envelope with a traditional thank-you card. Computer-savvy mamas can add a speech bubble to the picture to make the baby say, "Thanks for the hand-knit blanket, Aunt Shirley. It's totally not itchy!"

#97 *"Pair" down your shoe collection.*

Find, evaluate, admire, and throw away your shoes. This is a satisfying naptime activity.

Your goal is to get reacquainted with some old friends, walk down memory lane, then donate your least-favorite pairs to charity. Arrange your collection into rows and columns, arranged by color or style. Pluck one pair from each row for the donation pile.

If your shoe-grid is massive, you may need to cross-reference or work with a librarian to get through the task.

#98 Let your baby ride the family pet.

Someday your baby will be an adult. When that time comes, your pet will fit in your kid's lap.

But for now, isn't it hilarious to take pictures that really show how teeny-weeny your munchkin is? Take some pictures of your baby riding the family pet.

Make sure you follow commonsense tips for pet safety. But it's your dog/cat/llama/snake/etc., so we shouldn't have to tell you that.

#99 *Come out of your shell.*

Have you been a little hard to reach? It might be time to stop being such a hermit. Get a hands-free phone to catch up with friends while strolling or nursing, or make the time for a phone call during naptime.

Some of your friends might be scared to call because they think you're too busy or overwhelmed. Call them instead. You don't need an invitation.

#100 *Create a comic strip.*

Choose 3–5 photographs to assemble into a little story. Get some thought-bubble stickers intended for scrapbooking and have fun. Sure, this is cute for your baby, but keep in mind that you have a life (or at least you used to) with friends or siblings. Feature some of them in your comic strip, too.

Post the finished artwork on your refrigerator. It will remind all your guests how witty you are.

#101 *Sweat in your home gym.*

If you can't justify having a gym membership (and there are so many wonderful excuses available!), you can still set yourself up with a way to exercise while baby is napping or playing next to you. If you want to stretch, build strength, or get a little sweaty, find a way to make it happen in your living room or garage.

PICK SOME FAVORITE EXERCISES
.... FROM THESE SUGGESTIONS ....

- ★ **Stretch with resistance bands.** They're small, cheap, and versatile.
- ★ **Do step routines on real-live steps.**
- ★ **Buy a postnatal yoga DVD or two.** Now really use them.
- ★ **Turn your seldom-used bicycle into a stationary bike.**
- ★ **Bench-press your baby.**
- ★ **Lie on your back and imitate the baby until you get tired.** Amazing how they do all that kicking, huh?

#102 *Star in a webcast.*

Show your distant relatives what handling the baby is really like.

You can buy a webcam for about $40, and some new computers even have one built in. Buy one for the grandparents as well, if you want to see their smiling faces. Or, let baby watch herself on the screen; it doesn't require any special hardware on grandma and grandpa's end. Then, use an instant messenger program to host a private video-conference call, with your little squirt as the star. She may be adorable and make faces, she may try to flip out of your arms, or she may cry her head off. So much better than a still photo! Grandparents, uncles, and aunts will be delighted.

#103 *Tag along with a veteran mom.*

If you have a friend with a 2- or 3-year-old, or even 2 children, ask to shadow her for a few hours. Let her laugh at your rookie neuroses. Ask her questions. Learn from her.

#104 *Kick-off some family traditions.*

Yep, you're the parent here. Do you have fond childhood memories that you want to re-create with your new family? How about your mate? You may find yourself carrying on old family traditions, or you may even realize that you're trying to compensate for experiences you feel you missed out on. But worry not, and work out the details as you go along.

We both have our own odd traditions: Heather, who is not Jewish, is so fond of Hanukah traditions that she throws a Pot-Latke every year to celebrate. Whitney, who is Jewish, takes Julian to an annual Easter egg hunt with her childhood friends.

Conveniently, starting a new tradition before your kid turns 3 and starts to actually file away memories means that she'll think this is How It's Always Been. So if you don't get it together this year, you can try again next year.

#105 *High kick, spin, and flail for your biggest fan.*

Soon enough, you may be bullied into playing nonstop "kid's music," but before that happens, you can (and should!) sing and dance around to your favorite songs. It's great fun for you, and it can be good exercise if you keep it up long enough.

#106 *Be in love.*

Scrounge around for some pictures of you and your mate together from back when you first started out. Make a collage on the computer (if you know how) or do it the old-fashioned way, with tape and scissors. Put your collage on the fridge to remind you of your pre-baby lives.

Extra points if you can tie this activity to a birthday, Valentine, or anniversary occasion.

#107 *Crochet a simple hat.*

Wee little hats are so cute, and they're easy to make once you get into the groove. Crocheting doesn't require much equipment—just one hook and a ball of yarn—and a baby hat is just about the simplest thing you can make. If you have the patience, find a pattern online, and try your hand at a hat.

This activity is a good excuse to a) visit a yarn store, b) spend time with an older person who can teach you the basics or refresh your memory, and c) buy some really cute ribbon or buttons with which to embellish your finished hat.

Mini-hats also make good gifts and will have people scratching their heads asking, "Where do you find the time?" (The answer: during naptime, and while I half-watched my little one eat lint off the carpet.)

Month

6

#108 *Dump your purse.*

Spill it. What's in that thing? Anything slimy? Anything that would embarrass your former (cooler) self?

No matter how stylish your purse may be, we're guessing there's something unnecessary in it. Dump it on your kitchen counter and make a pile for "put away," "throw away," and "back in the purse." Or, just laugh at yourself and reload.

#109 *Check out the library.*

Since it seems like you can find just about all the information you'll ever need on the Internet, it's easy to wonder who actually uses the library any more. But once you have a baby, the answer is you.

If you haven't done so already, we highly recommend that you and your little one visit your local library for the baby and toddler story time. It's pretty great — someone else entertains your baby with a new voice and stories while you just space out and relax. But, hey, be on time. If you're 5 minutes late, you'll miss half.

As long as you're already there, check out a few board books, big-kid books, learning-to-sign DVDs, and video rentals for grown-ups. With so many unavoidable parenting expenses, it's nice to go someplace where it's all free. And air conditioned.

#110 *Act like Julie from* **The Love Boat.**

It's time to make your own fun. Plan your week and write up the schedule. Pick an activity and a time and tell everyone available that they're welcome to join you. Be brave and invite folks you hardly know. Or send an e-mail with your whole week's agenda to get your friends excited about the fun you're going to have in the next seven days. You are the cruise director. Your friends will thank you later.

.... **HERE ARE SOME IDEAS TO GET YOU STARTED** ....

- ★ **Monday:** Pack up the kiddo and meet a friend for a walk; look for doggies and other babies. Treat yourself to a cupcake afterward.
- ★ **Tuesday:** Find a baby matinee movie to enjoy with friends. Take turns watching each other's snoozing babies so that you can go to the bathroom—*alone*!
- ★ **Wednesday:** Stretch at a mom-and-baby yoga class, followed by tea and meditative breathing.
- ★ **Thursday:** Visit the bookstore and pet shop; grab take-out for dinner.
- ★ **Friday:** Play in a neighborhood playground, then treat yourself to a mocha at a café.
- ★ **Saturday:** Take a stroller or backpack hike around a hilly park, then have a picnic.
- ★ **Sunday:** Host a backyard play date. Ask everyone to bring a toy to ease your burden as host.

#111 *Promise yourself a rose garden.*

Find a nearby botanical garden and meet a single friend for a relaxed walk. With the baby strapped to your chest and facing outward, he can enjoy the sights and smells along with you. Try to trick your friend into thinking that babies are all sunshine and roses.

#112 *Cook like you're feeding the Huxtable family.*

Next time you go through the effort to cook, double the recipe and freeze half. Make sure you freeze portions you'll actually want to use. It's a real bummer to spend forever defrosting an entire brick of beef stew because you can't chisel off the right amount for two adults. Pretty soon, you'll be able to make and freeze food for your baby, too (see page 128 for tips on homemade baby food).

.... **SOME IDEAS FOR MEALS TO COOK AND FREEZE** ....

★ Lasagna ★ Beef stew ★ Veggie chili ★
★ Homemade mac and cheese ★ Soup ★
★ Any casserole or masterpiece from your crock pot ★

#113 Plan an overnight getaway with another family.

Here's the thing: When you go out of town as just-the-family and the baby goes to bed before 8 P.M., the rest of the evening can be oppressively quiet for you and your partner — and sadly not too different from evenings you already spend together at home.

One answer to this dilemma is to recruit another trio to go on a trip so that you can continue to socialize with grown-ups once the little people are asleep. Morning is also more fun — your early-rising party of six can hit a popular restaurant before it gets crowded.

#114 *Use the Internet for errands.*

We all know it's not cool to leave the house while your baby sleeps, but you can still use those snippets of naptime to get lots of things done. We both had a penchant for online shopping before becoming moms, so it's natural that we've taken it one step further.

.... **HERE ARE SOME ACTIVITIES WE DO ONLINE** ....

* **Pay bills.** Most banks offer online account management and bill paying. Avoid those silly banker hours and manage your finances on your own time.
* **Buy stamps.** The U.S. Postal Service Web site will take stamp orders online and send them directly to your house. Same goes for the postal services in Canada, the United Kingdom, and many other countries.
* **Stock up on diapers.** Shopping online for diapers allows you to compare prices before you buy.
* **"Window" shop.** Ahh, yes. The allure of shopping without dealing with crowds is a great joy to rookie moms—and it's that much better when your little one is asleep.
* **Buy food.** Many local and chain grocery stores offer delivery service. It can take a few times to get it right (for example, once Heather bought mini bread instead of normal bread because they looked the same size in the picture on the Web site). But it's worth it to have someone else carry the groceries to your door.

#115 *Spend more time in bed.*

Remember that first month, when it took all your energy to get out of your pajamas? Well, now that several months have gone by, we think you should stay in them.

Focus one day this week on getting more rest. Don't get out of your PJs in the morning, jumping right back in bed as soon as you put the baby down for a nap. If you can't fall asleep, read a magazine. During baby's next naptime, take a shower and then get back in bed. If you can't fall asleep, talk on the phone. In bed.

If you're a stay-at-home mom, this day can be a weekday. If you're a working mom, show this chapter to your partner and enjoy a weekend in bed. Heck, if your baby-daddy is home, he can get you breakfast in bed during that morning nap. And then he can join you. Yum.

#116 *Heighten the contrast of your photos.*

Have you taken black and white photos of your baby yet?

Lay her on a solid-color blanket on your bed and take some shots from varied vantage points: above, below, straight on. Next, get down at her level and take some close-ups. Shoot some pictures of her hands and feet, too.

To make an outing of it, take that blanket with you and start snapping on your patio, in the backyard, or at a local park. Outdoor light makes for great black and white pictures.

#117 *Order from a waiter.*

Hit a restaurant with your partner and baby on a weeknight. Blowing your baby's bedtime occasionally isn't going to hurt anyone. If you think your baby just cannot make it through the meal, put him back in the ol' bucket-seat stroller and roll him to sleep, like you did in the early days.

If you're afraid you'll feel embarrassed by crying, go to a family restaurant. Seriously, you're a family now.

#118 *Give your back a break.*

Ask a friend or sibling if they want to "wear the baby" while you're out and about. Friends without babies love to wear the front carrier. Let them. Six-month-olds are heavy!

Arrange for someone to meet you at the shopping center. Once the baby is strapped on tightly to your trusted assistant, your hands will be free to pick up clothes, take them to the dressing room, try them on, and pay for them. None of this would be pleasant with the weight of a baby on your shoulders.

#119 *Take in an outdoor rock concert.*

Do you miss the days of following Phish all summer long? Or maybe you loved going to the symphony with your folks as a child?

Wait for a mild day, pack a blanket and a picnic, and take your baby to an outdoor show. Yes, it will be harder than going with friends, but it's so much fun and well worth the effort. The sounds will drown out any crying coming from your blanket area, and the fresh air will mask stinky smells emanating from your diaper bag.

#120 *Decorate baby clothes with fabric paint.*

If you want to hang out with us, please don't go all crazy freehand with puffy paint on your baby's clothes (unless you're dressing your baby for an '80s party). Instead, choose a stencil to achieve a cleaner and more modern look:

1 Buy fabric paint and thin, bendable, plastic stencils from a craft store. They come in varied shapes. (If you're very clever, make your own template with an X-acto knife and freezer paper.)

2 Place wax paper directly below the layer of fabric. If it's a shirt, slip the wax paper inside.

3 Hold the template firmly and use a paintbrush or sponge brush to apply the fabric paint. We recommend using a limited palette, for example, no more than three colors on one item of clothing.

4 Remove the template and admire your handiwork.

#121 *Volunteer with your baby.*

Two groups who love babies are senior citizens and grade-school children. Find a crew that needs your help with reading stories and go visit them.

#122 *Drive by your hospital.*

Put your cranky kid into the car and drive him to sleep this afternoon. Make your way to the hospital where your pediatrician has admitting rights. In an emergency, you don't want to be trying to figure out directions, and in many cases, your pediatrician is associated with a hospital other than the one in which your baby was born.

This is not the first driving suggestion we've made, so we must apologize to any rookie moms whose babies do nothing but scream in their car seats. Who knows, though. Today could be your lucky day.

#123 *Host a movie night.*

You can't go to the movies as often as you once did, but you can still make a social event out of seeing one. Get on the phone with some friends and go through a list of new-to-DVD videos you want to see. Once you all agree on one, choose a start time that's about thirty minutes after your baby's bedtime. And since your friends are coming to you, put yourself in charge of supplying the candy, popcorn, and soda.

#124 *Hop in a photo booth.*

Stick your baby's head in a photo booth. Hold him steady and watch the different expressions unfold. If the first batch is dull, try again with funny hats.

#125 Be a dad for a day.

Take a cue from dads everywhere and do something a little different with your baby today. Unfamiliar destinations engage your baby and make him watchful.

Go somewhere you don't usually take the baby—the hardware store, a new convenience store, the dry cleaners. You get the idea. Use different gear, too: Try the backpack, the jogging stroller, or the wagon. Some dads practice guitar, play fantasy sports online, or just watch TV in front of their captive little audiences. What's really so terrible about these habits?

Or ask your partner what you could do that would be more like him. Stay-at-home moms, ask your partner what he'd do today if he were you.

#126 Party like you have a 6-month-old.

Plan a Mom's Night Out with some girlfriends to celebrate your 6-month milestone. Go somewhere you used to enjoy in your old life. Indulge in a new restaurant, visit a favorite bar, or just see a movie together. Ask your partner in advance to cover the morning shift so you can sleep in a little.

Learning to Crawl

MONTHS 7 THROUGH 9

Sometimes it feels like your baby is another limb, a part of your body that's permanently attached. The good news is that she's not. You can actually share the responsibility of caring for her with other people! This will free you up to do some adult activities and carry fewer bags everywhere you go.

.... YOUR NEW SKILLS ....

* ★ Making your baby laugh
* ★ Reciting board books from memory
* ★ Folding more laundry than Alice on The Brady Bunch
* ★ Introducing yourself to other women with strollers

.... YOUR NEW FEARS ....

* ★ You're turning into a boring person with no interests other than babies
* ★ You're missing important milestones while you're away from your baby
* ★ You're not feeding your baby the right foods at the right time

Now that your baby is rolling, scooting, or crawling, she isn't staying where you left her. Luckily, babies make good dance partners, and they're still too young to be embarrassed by your off-key singing and hastily thrown-together outfits. If you're not headed to the gym, it's time to step away from the sweatpants. Wear cute shoes and revive your old interests. Start looking for the old you that had a full life, even without a baby. We'll help you find her.

Month

7

#127 *Upgrade your own "crib."*

You probably did nice things to your baby's bedroom to get it ready for her. But what about yours?

Make a small change that will refresh your bedroom. Move a piece of furniture, hang something on the wall, go wild painting an accent wall, or get rid of a clutter pile. (Note: We didn't say clean up—just hide it somewhere else!)

#128 *Fondle the veggies at a farmer's market.*

Find a local farmer's market to visit. Look around and choose a vegetable your baby hasn't tried yet. Bring it home, steam it, puree or mash it with a fork, and introduce your baby to a new flavor.

Doesn't sound like enough action for you? Believe us, it is. Navigating a stroller through the market area is a challenge, and there are so many things for your baby to look at that you'll find it worth the effort.

#129 Say "Yes, thank you."

Do you tell people "No, thank you" when they offer to help? Start letting them. You'll make them feel good, too.

Think of things that you feel comfortable asking others to do so that when they offer, you can accept their generosity. During the course of the day, say them out loud to your baby to help you remember.

.... **EXAMPLE CONVERSATION** ....

- ★ **Baby:** Daaaaa da daaa da uh ga
- ★ **You:** Someone needs to take the car for an oil change.
- ★ **Baby:** Dahhh shhsss da
- ★ **You:** Yes, I would love some Indian take-out for dinner.
- ★ **Baby:** ssshhss ah babababababa
- ★ **You:** The lawn does need to be mowed.

#130 *Camp out.*

Play outside; enjoy the stars; sleep in a tent; and rise with the sun. Babies can really enjoy the experience when their parents are the outdoorsy type.

Do a practice campout in your backyard or living room. If camping isn't your thing, just leave it at that. This close-to-home version can be its own adventure.

If you're a hardcore camper who's been reluctant to get back on the trails with baby in tow, there is no shame in car camping. The convenience of being able to bring an unlimited amount of baby gear cannot be overestimated. We both have huge family-sized tents that can accommodate a portable crib. There's no way we'd hike anywhere with those things on our backs, but for sleeping a few feet from our car, they're perfect.

Take your camping trip with other friends (with or without kids) so that you have someone else to hang out with around the campfire.

#131 *Let baby dress herself.*

We've always admired the 3-year-olds we see around town dressed in wild combinations of cowboy boots, gingham, rainbow tights, and superhero capes. Do you wonder when your own baby will wear such creative and charming combinations?

Liven up your infant's outfit. If your baby is grabbing, she's capable of picking out her own clothes. Start at the bottom and work up:

1 **Let baby "select" from 2 or 3 pairs of socks.** The idea is that she wears whichever ones she touches (grabbing or sucking is OK, too).

2 **Allow her to pick from 2 shirts.**

3 **Let her pick pants, hats, and other accessories.**

Now you can brag that baby picked out her own clothes. And at least you'll get a good laugh about it, even if nobody else seems to care.

#132 *Run, mommy, run!*

If you like to run or walk with a partner (and really want to get back out there), what are you waiting for? Rookie mom Amanda runs with 5 other women in her neighborhood. They meet outside at 6:30 A.M. to get going, leaving their partners on duty for the next hour.

THERE ARE MANY PLACES TO FIND
.... **YOUR PERFECTLY PACED COMPANION** ....

★ **Ask your old buddies if they want to walk before work.**

★ **Use the Internet.** Check out www.SeeMommyRun.com to find a group in your area, or start your own group by posting an ad on a mom's-group Web site (for example, www.MothersClick.com).

★ **Enlist your partner.** Pull out the jogging stroller and commit to regular walking or running together as a family.

#133 *Seek friendly baby-proofing advice.*

When it comes to baby-proofing, experienced friends are your most valuable resource. Ask someone who has a toddler to walk around your house, room by room, pointing out all the little hazards her mommy mind can count. Take notes. Alternatives are to set a 13-month-old loose in your house and correct everything she gets into. But that could be a lot messier!

Now for some perspective. This may sound dramatic, but your first priorities should be to fix the things that could kill your baby. Dangers that might result in only small injuries or minor damages to your home decor are your second priorities. Example: First move the TV so it won't fall on baby (possibly fatal), then move the plant that could tip over onto the floor (not fatal, just messy).

#134 *Use your baby as a bumper sticker.*

What better way to call people's attention to your beliefs than to plaster catchy slogans on your precious peanut? Name your cause and there's likely some matching baby apparel available online. If you're cheap (like we are), you can always improvise with your own iron-ons or a Sharpie.

#135 *Sew some easy kids pants.*

Read carefully and you will learn how to transform one of your husband's discarded T-shirts into a pair of comfy baby-sized pants, perfect for napping and crawling. There are only 3 seams to sew, so even if you don't have a machine, you can probably accomplish this task by hand.

.... **WHAT YOU NEED** ....

★ Large T-shirt, ideally in a vibrant color or with a fun pattern ★
★ Scissors ★ Marking pen ★ Enough elastic to go around your baby's waist ★
★ Rookie sewing skills ★

1 **Fold a pair of your baby's pants in half,** with the crotch sticking out.

2 **Use the folded pants as a template.** Lay your T-shirt flat, then place the folded pants on the shirt, aligning the bottom hem of the pants with the bottom hem of shirt and the left side of the shirt with the outside of the pants. The crotch of the pants should face inward, toward the middle of the shirt. Use the marker to trace around the pants on the shirt, adding about a quarter inch for a seam allowance.

3 **Trace a mirror image of first shape on the other side of the T-shirt.** You'll need to turn the pants to face the other direction, so the crotch remains facing inward.

4 **Cut out both shapes.**

5 **Place the unfolded pant legs on top of one another,** with the right sides of the material facing in. You'll have a curved slope on each outer edge.

6 **Pin the two pieces together along the curves, then sew them together.** Without a sewing machine, you'll want to use a small running stitch or a backstitch, if you know what that is.

7 **Refold your pants** so the curves you just sewed together are in the middle rather than on the edge. You'll see that you have created a pair of pants that simply need the inseams sewn up. Sew the inseams.

8 **Fold the waist over about an inch and sew around it.** Leave a hole through which you can insert a piece of elastic.

9 **Pull the elastic through the casing you've created in the waist.** Fasten a safety pin to the end of the elastic to make it easier to thread through. Use a few stitches to sew the ends of the elastic together, close the hole in the waist, and you're done! (For tiny babies who don't move, you can skip the elastic altogether.)

#136 Watch the car from afar.

Whether you do it on purpose (driving around town to induce a nap) or by accident (windows down, music blaring, begging baby to stay awake to no avail), sooner or later your baby will fall asleep in the car. Sure, you'll be delighted to see the blissed-out look of baby sleep, but you might also wonder what the #*&! to do with yourself in the car for 45 minutes.

Those of you with a driveway or parking lot can set up a car-watching station. If you can see the car from your porch, hang out there and keep an eye and ear on the car. Or keep a lawn chair in the trunk, along with a stash of magazines or a book. Just remember to open the windows and periodically monitor the temperature in the car. Instead of being frustrated, think of the unexpected gift of time you've just been given!

#137 Hop in the shower with your partner.

Put your baby to bed and get wet. Need more instructions? We didn't think so.

#138 *Try anything and everything for 4 days.*

We all get superstitious about what works and doesn't work with our babies. We have even referred to a pair of pajamas as "lucky," believing they have the power to make the baby sleep longer. Then when our talismans don't work, we get discouraged.

Have patience! When you're trying something new, whether it's a new bedtime, bottle, or feeding routine, stick with it for at least 4 days before writing it off (or on).

#139 *Sharpen your brain.*

Have you noticed that the baby brain you developed during pregnancy has not really improved much? Well, you can blame it on your lack of sleep and obsessive need to tune in to your baby's diaper status.

Try to find a few minutes today for a word jumble, Sudoku, or crossword puzzle or see how many words you can make out of "I still got it, baby." If you can manage, read the non-game pages of the newspaper as a bonus.

#140 *Cook in someone else's kitchen (and don't clean up).*

Still having trouble getting dinner on the table? You're not alone! Thankfully, there are people out there who understand our problem. Services are popping up all over to help us out. (No, not McDonald's.)

Meal-preparation companies offer you an opportunity to sign up for cooking sessions in a professional kitchen, where you assemble fresh, tasty meals and leave with dozens of packages to place in your freezer. And someone else does the shopping, prep, and cleanup! Sound too good to be true? We've done this quite a few times, and it's practically perfect. Do an Internet search for "meal preparation" and the name of your town to find this service in your area.

#141 *Document examples of bad parenting.*

Do you let your baby hold your beer bottle, just to get a cheap laugh? How about putting her in the driver's seat of the car so she can turn the steering wheel?

Take a series of photos that demonstrate "What Not to Do" and share them with your partner and parents for a laugh.

#142 Go out for just dessert.

We're assuming that we're not the only rookie moms for whom leaving the baby to be put to bed by a babysitter is scary. Whitney's kid never accepted a bottle, so she pretty much had to be there for bedtime nursing for the first 10 months. This feeling is the opposite of freedom, by the way.

But once your baby is reliably sleeping between 8 P.M. and midnight or beyond, you can resume the life you used to lead by making dessert dates with girlfriends or your partner. This is the least stressful babysitter situation possible. Pretty much anyone is qualified to lie on your couch and watch TV while you enjoy an evening outing, right?

Here's what you do: Put your baby to bed the way you like. When you're confident she's asleep, head out to any of your favorite restaurants. Order dessert or a drink. Enjoy the ambience. Go home.

#143 *Take a hike.*

Put your big baby in a backpack carrier and hike around. Just do yourself a favor and make your first carrier-laden hike a quick jaunt around the house or yard, just in case you or baby hate this new method of transport. When you're ready, hit the real world for some hands-free walking or take a real hike through actual nature!

#144 *Shoot the kids.*

Rack 'em, stack 'em, photograph 'em.

Each time there are two or more babies around, put them on the couch and photograph the lineup. Who knows who might go to the prom together one day?

#145 Finagle a free portrait.

All the big photo chains want to hook you on their services. If they can get you to love the pictures and buy huge packages, you'll probably go back there every 6 months, as your baby ages. Why not sample a little before you buy? Track down a coupon online and make your outing of the day a professional photo shoot. Call ahead to make sure they have room for you in the schedule.

Don't feel bad taking advantage of one of the free offers. Most of us won't be able to resist buying a few extras. But if the picture isn't great, just go home with your freebie.

A word of advice: Put a bib on your baby before you leave the house, and don't take it off until the photographer is ready to shoot.

#146 Be a selfish June Cleaver.

You can appear to be super generous when you bake something and take it over to a friend's house. But if you're smart, you've doubled the recipe and kept half for yourself.

So next time you're headed over to see a new baby, consider which treat you'd rather eat: banana bread or ginger snaps. Then make two batches and enjoy the fruits of your labor.

#147 Blend your own baby food.

Take some fresh fruits and vegetables and puree them with breast milk or formula to the right consistency. Did we just scare you with too many assumptions about your kitchen savvy? Ok, baby steps. Let's start with the most basic:

1 **Boil some water.** You do know how to boil water, right?
2 **Slice some pears and add them to the boiling water.**
3 **When they are soft (probably about 2 minutes), remove them from the water.**
4 **Put the soft pears in that food-processor thingy or blender.**
5 **Now turn it on.**
6 **Transfer the mixture to a baby bowl and check the thickness.**

You can do this with many foods, including meats. When you use a heartier food like sweet potatoes, you may want to thin the mixture with water, breast milk, or formula. When you're comfortable with the single ingredients, try combinations, like apples and squash or chicken and apricots.

Do you feel like Supermom? We advise you to make and freeze as much as you can while you still have the interest and energy. This novel activity may lose its appeal as your baby gets older and moves around more.

Month

8

#148 Squeeze in brunch.

Find a good time between baby's naps to enjoy brunch in a restaurant with your partner or friends.

Criteria should include more than just delicious food: You want to find a place without fancy tablecloths, with a changing table in the restroom, and with enough space between tables that you can wheel a stroller or carry both baby and diaper bag without whacking fellow diners. Ambient noise is generally a big plus!

#149 Split your movie night.

Given the high price of a babysitter and what they're charging for movies these days, it's hard to imagine a cheap evening date. So, consider doing what Heather and her husband did: Go see a new-release movie while your partner stays home with the baby; return home and then stay with the baby while your partner goes to a later showing of the same film. Then discuss it together at home, where the ice cream is free.

#150 Swap baby food like trading cards.

If you're up for making some good, fresh baby food, hold a food swap with some other mom friends to introduce your kid to new flavors. You'll broaden her palate while reducing your own effort and shopping! Here's how:

1 Make a huge batch of sweet potatoes or winter squash. If you forget how to do this, check out activity #147 on page 126 for a refresher.

2 Your pals, Bertha and Hildegard, make a huge batch of lentils and stewed pears.

3 Give some of your sweet potatoes to Big B and Miz H.

4 Open your arms to receive lentils and pears from them.

5 When you get home put the fresh and tasty mush in ice cube trays, freeze into little food cubes, and store in labeled resealable freezer bags. Voilà! All 3 babes have some new foods to learn about.

Experiment with combinations of fruits and vegetables.

.... Our favorites ....
★ Squash/Pear ★ Carrot/Apple ★ Pear/Mango/Banana ★ Carrot/Sweet Potato ★

.... Our worst experiences ....
★ Green Beans/Tofu ★ Carrot/Parsnip ★

#151 Walk an extra mile.

Did you listen to us in activity #46 when we told you to get yourself a pedometer? Well, if you didn't do it then, do it now. Having a pedometer makes a walk more enjoyable because it's a way to get credit for your effort. It's like you're in a video game collecting points, but the points are good for you.

Today's pedometer assignment: Double your average steps. You might have to take an extra walk to accomplish this goal—maybe even a stroll by yourself when your partner gets home from work. Yes, you can take a walk in the dark. Just stick to well-traveled routes and wear white. If that doesn't sound like it will work for you, then take an extra-long walk with babe in the afternoon.

#152 Give handmade gifts.

We see so many cute things in gift shops that we could make ourselves. How about a beaded necklace? A baby-sized sweatshirt with a patch sewn on? A wallet made from duct tape?

Take yourself to a craft store and get inspired. Use the Web to find a tutorial for making something a little different.

We promise—giving a gift you create yourself does not make you look like a 5-year-old; it makes you look like a renaissance woman.

#153 *Play a different role.*

To break out of your normal routine, plan a silly adults-only outing, complete with funny costumes. Try to get a flock of friends to play along.

One rookie mom we know accepted a dare and went to the movies with underwear on her head.

Variation: Ask your honey to meet you at a bar after work and show up in an outrageous disguise (way sluttier than your normal wardrobe). Try to pick him up. Be over-the-top with your flirtations while trying to keep a straight face.

#154 *Snap out of it!*

If you've been pretty good about establishing a consistent evening and bedtime routine, it's time to shake things up. Stop refusing invitations to dinner parties; instead, ask if you can bring your baby and a portable crib.

Pack up your baby's PJs and feeding supplies for an evening of reckless abandon. Execute your nighttime routine in a friend's unfamiliar bedroom with the on-the-road comforts of your porta-crib. Or, even crazier, blow bedtime outright and let your baby fall asleep in his daddy's arms like a 2-month-old.

With practice, you may well encourage some flexibility in your child. Yay!

#155 *Bathe with your baby.*

The bouncy seat will be your best friend on this adventure. Here are instructions for taking a bath with baby, in 3 easy stages.

.... Stage I: PREP ....

1 Throw your towels in the dryer for a few minutes for that (optional) spa experience. Grab a robe if you have one.

2 Place a bouncy seat next to the tub. Remove any hanging toy or activity bar.

3 Fill the tub with water of a comfortable temperature.

4 Gather the rest of the necessary stuff. Grab washcloths and toys.

5 Strip your baby and lay her towel over the bouncy seat.

6 Place her there while you step into the tub, then lift her in, too.

.... Stage II: DURING ....

1 Hug, cuddle, and sing.

2 Wash baby as much as is practical.

.... Stage III: AFTER ....

1 Gently place your baby on the warmed towel in the bouncy seat.

2 Step out and into your own towel.

3 Hug and cuddle some more.

4 Put on your robe to make dressing the baby easier.

#156 *Alter your board books.*

When Whitney had a board book she wasn't crazy about, she took matters into her own crafty little hands. The book she was willing to sacrifice featured washed-out pastel illustrations and too many words. She prefers bold pictures and simple text. Plus funny. So, she used the skeleton of the first book to make a board book that suited her taste.

To alter your own board book, first coat all the pages, including the cover, with nontoxic paint. When it's dry, use letter stickers or go freehand to add your own title to the cover. Use the inside pages to tell a story or, like many board books, simply teach vocabulary with big pictures and subtitles.

Whitney made a cartoonlike image of her husband's head and copied enough for each page. Then she placed the head in various environments cut out of magazines. She handwrote the captions.

Don't worry about letting the original contents of the book show through. Its handmade quality is part of your new board book's charm.

#157 *Swap 'til you drop.*

Invite your most stylish friends and acquaintances to a clothing-swap party at your place. Urge them to purge their closets and bring everything they don't want, from exercise clothes to cocktail dresses. Clean clothes should be brought to your house in big shopping bags. Then set aside a good hour and sort through your own closet. Be brutal. If you're feeling those pesky postpartum body issues, get a good friend to help you. (Do your marriage the small favor of not asking your husband if your "butt looks big in this"!)

To prepare, clean and fold your offerings for the swap. Then prep your party space. Make sure you have a mirror handy, and if you have room, "merchandise" your stuff to make it a little more fun to "shop." Use the computer or write on

index cards to indicate categories of clothing so that guests can sort their offerings ("Pants Size 8 and Under," "Sexy Tops," "Work Dresses"). Keep a few blank labels nearby for catagories that emerge during the course of the party. Who knew that your friends had so many never-used "Beach Cover-Ups?"

The actual party is a breeze—the whole thing can be over in less than 2 hours. Tidy up before everyone arrives, wear cute underwear, buy some appetizers (or ask your friends to bring them), and wait for everyone to bring you new clothes!

At Heather's annual swapping party, we usually start out browsing the piles casually and trying stuff on here and there. After that, the claws come out: Once you try on a cute spangly dress, it's fair game for someone else to have a go at it. Let your friends decide who really looks best in it.

There will be bags and bags of leftovers that no one wants. Get someone to help you load the car and then take the bags directly to a donation center.

THE THREE CHIEF BENEFITS
.... OF A CLOTHING-SWAP PARTY ....

1   It will force you to step away from your ill-fitting clothes and rein-
    vigorate your wardrobe on the cheap.
2   When you let Daddy take the babe out for a hike, you'll get a little
    girl time with your friends.
3   It generates a hefty clothing donation that can benefit women in need.

#158 Stumble into a family-friendly pub.

You don't have to compromise on ambiance every time you go out for dinner with your baby. You want a beer after work (or after spending the day alone together), and your baby wants to bang spoons on the table. No problem.

Bars that serve food also service babies. Many of them have noise levels that will enable your family to blend right in. So don't be afraid: Go to a sports bar or an Irish pub. Pull up a high chair and get rowdy with the rest of the crowd.

#159 Introduce the Tupperware.

Give your baby access to plastic storage containers in your kitchen. If you're not already storing them on a bottom shelf, swap cabinets so they're within reach. Then sit on the kitchen floor together and let her pull everything off the shelf and bang it around.

This new cabinet full of toys may even allow you to spend some quality time together while you're fixing dinner or a snack.

#160 *Get your baby a job as a scientist.*

If you live in a college town, your baby may have the opportunity to contribute to important research. Psychology and child-development labs are often looking for infants to take part in studies. Call the appropriate department and ask if they have any such opportunities.

.... **WANTED! UNEMPLOYED BABIES** ....
Here are a few other careers your baby might like to pursue:

★ **Baby doll:** Seek out an expecting couple you know and offer to let them practice on your baby. Suggest they give her a bath, then go do something else during the bath so you don't act like a total control freak and scare your friends.

★ **Usability tester:** Contact toy companies to find out if they have any testing programs.

★ **Actor/Model:** If you live in Los Angeles or New York City, now is the time to force your child into showbiz.

★ **Cheerleader:** Dress your baby in a college team outfit and take her to a sporting event. Let the team interpret her screaming as cheers.

★ **Paperweight:** If baby is not yet crawling, place her on a stack of papers.

#161 *Purge your crap the easy way.*

Today, while your little sidekick enjoys some private time with an annoying musical toy, you will be studying your house and its contents.

1 Select 3 things to throw away in each room. Put them all in a trash bag. Don't forget the trunk of your car, your entryway, and laundry room.

2 Select 3 things to donate from each room. Put all those things into another trash bag.

3 Finally, walk your house with a bag and fill it with things you're not ready to part with (i.e., things you should have tossed on the first 2 passes). Put the bag in storage in the garage, attic, or shed.

4 Repeat monthly.

#162 *Play with someone else's toys.*

Seven months old and bored already? The nerve of some people.

If it seems that everyone else's toys are more fun, find another mom to trade with. Agree to a specific trade period (for example, 2 weeks) and then trade back.

If you hang with a bigger posse, organize a toy swap. For the next play date, ask everyone to bring something that her child is bored with and then send everyone home with something different. You can trade back (or swap again) the next time you get together.

This activity is especially recommended for moms who are taking their little ones on an airplane. Keep the new toy hidden until you're on the plane, then bust it out when you need a distraction. You'll keep the kid busy for at least 2 extra minutes. The rest of the time, you're on your own.

#163 *Indulge in a spa day.*

Heather got a gift certificate for a massage as a "congrats for pushing that baby out" from a good friend, but baby Holden was 10 months old before she got her tired butt into the spa. Don't do that to yourself. You deserve it now. Put your partner on baby duty and book a couple hours of relaxation for yourself (or with friends). Get a massage or a facial or whatever feels great to you. Go on, do it. Happy birth day to you.

#164 Sign with your baby.

Once your baby can wave "hello," she can begin signing other things, too. Start signing a few things consistently now (Whitney started with "more" and "eat" and "milk"), and within a few months your baby will likely start to respond by doing them back. The signs will help you communicate with each other as your baby develops verbal skills.

Our number one favorite baby sign is "help," which is performed by tapping both hands against the chest. This sign really comes in handy when baby needs help with a toy or to reach something that she just shoved under the couch, and it's much more civilized than pointing and grunting.

Learn more about baby sign language with a book, Web site, or DVD.

#165 *Make a cheap-o rattle.*

If the word *free* starts your mouth watering, then we have something in common. Who doesn't like to have a new toy without spending money? Best of all, Heather found that Holden chose the faux rattle she invented above all his usual toys, rolling it and shaking it for 2 days straight. Here's how to make this awe-inspiring plaything:

1 **Wash and remove the label from a small plastic container.** Use a container from juice or another food.

2 **Let the container dry completely.**

3 **Insert about 6 pieces of macaroni.** For a louder rattle, use pennies (still cheap—just 6 cents!).

4 **Thoroughly tape the container shut** with duct tape or sturdy, clear packaging tape. (You'll thank us later when your baby is not choking on pennies or pasta.)

5 **Leave the rattle out for baby to discover.**

#166 *Throw an easy dinner party.*

Does the word *potluck* conjure up images of nasty casseroles from a bygone era? It doesn't have to. Throwing your own potluck is the perfect opportunity to experience an eclectic array of complementary taste sensations, with minimal prep and cleanup. Just invite some friends and distribute the responsibilities that go along with dinner. You'll have less to worry about and more fun all around.

.... **A FEW EASY GUIDELINES FOR YOUR FEAST** ....

★ **Choose a theme, if you're so inclined.**

★ **Assign parts of the meal by skill level.** (For example, ask your baker friend to bring dessert and your clueless-in-the-kitchen friend to bring drinks.) It's totally up to you whether you provide the main dish or farm that out to someone else, too.

★ **Eat on paper plates with plastic cutlery to minimize cleanup.**

★ **Send the dirty serving dishes home with their owners.**

#167 Buy or borrow a jogging stroller (but don't use it yourself).

Jogging strollers* seem to appeal to men; use this new gear to persuade your partner to go out for a jog with the baby so you can catch up on sleep, phone calls, or reading. Give Dad a bottle or pacifier to take on the trip to increase the chance of your little one staying calm and happy longer.

Even if you decide to trot alongside the two of them, let daddy push the stroller. If he's faster than you, the stroller-pushing job will help level the playing field.

* Check with your pediatrician for safety tips before using the jogging stroller for the first time.

#168 Take pictures of baby contortionism.

Can you easily clap your feet or suck on your own toes? Your baby can. Capture it on film for posterity.

#169 *Take your tot to a grown-up restaurant.*

Had enough of your standard family restaurants? Take a chance on a more refined venue. How will you know if it's possible if you don't try?

There are fancy restaurants with linen tablecloths and eerie, romantic silence, and then there are groovy, funky, (bustling (read:noisy) restaurants that make you feel like an adult again. Try taking your high-chair-sittin' baby to the latter.

Go out with a big noisy group when you can. Or at least go with understanding, kid-loving people who will want to give you and your spouse a break by taking the kid to look around. The meal will go more smoothly.

TIPS FOR A GOOD EVENING
·········· **AT AN ADULT DINING ESTABLISHMENT** ··········

★ **Pack the baby's favorite foods, spoons, and bibs.**

★ **Go early.** Don't mess with bedtime or long waits.

★ **Scope out an area for the kid to explore on hands and knees.**

★ **As soon as you've ordered, take the baby for a lap around the restaurant.** Return to the table when the food arrives.

★ **Cut up some of your food and share it with the babe.**

★ **Consider laying a napkin around the highchair to catch most of the shrapnel.**

★ **When baby is done eating, pass her around the table,** letting everyone have a few minutes with her.

Month

9

#170 E-mail your baby.

Let's face it: Handwriting in baby books is old school. Screen-based communication is what our kids will expect. That's how their lives will be documented.

Sign your kid up for an e-mail address so you can send messages to her future self. All those things you're not writing in the baby book are candidates for a note sent to your child's future inbox.

> **Dear Julian,** Today you threw a tantrum like none I have ever seen. You have impressed me.
>
> **Dear Holden,** Today you said "Mama" in a way that told me you knew exactly how to use that word.
>
> **Dear Scarlett,** I just took my first business trip away from you, and it wasn't half-bad.

If you're committed to the paper-based method, check baby's inbox from time to time and print out your messages. Or just wait. When these kids are old enough to open their inboxes for themselves, they can read all the notes you sent them when they were too young to understand. And hopefully they won't see your name in the "From" line and click "This is spam."

#171 *Say goodbye to mom shoes.*

It is a truth universally acknowledged that the quickest way to turn into your mother is to wear out-of-date shoes.

Wearing cute shoes will upgrade your whole outfit and make you feel better. They don't have to be high-heeled or pointy. Look for something that's casual, comfortable, *and* trendy.

Just because you're pushing a stroller doesn't mean you should be wearing white running shoes all around town. Leave that fashion faux pas for the grandmas.

#172 *Be a tourist in your own town.*

If you've never taken the time to see your hometown's greatest hits, go to a bookstore and pick up a local guide. Then choose a new destination and make a day of it. Seek out museums and activities where kids under 2 are admitted free. Even better, find a day with free admission for everyone and go with a girlfriend!

#173 *Find your celebrity baby match.*

Tori Spelling got married the same weekend as Heather, and they were pregnant at the same time, too. They are cosmically linked, whether Tori knows it or not! And Julia Roberts and Whitney were pregnant the same time, *twice*. . . .Whoa.

Were you pregnant at the same time as your favorite tabloid hussy? If you haven't already investigated your celebrity baby match, give it a go. Take pictures of your baby in similar outfits or situations as those you find in the press. Enjoy yourself now, and when your child is old enough to realize how crazy this makes you, you can all have a good laugh.

#174 *Blow bubbles.*

Bubbles can be a fantastic surprise for your baby. Pick up a bottle of bubble soap in the drug-store toy aisle. If you're lucky enough to find an older child nearby, ask if she would like to show the baby how bubbles are blown. Then sit back and watch the magic. Take the bottle with you in your diaper bag and pull out the bubbles whenever you need to provide baby with a distraction.

#175 Create a family photo wall.

Set up a family photo wall to help your little one learn his relative's faces. Asking family members to supply their own pictures will get the task done faster and avoid complaints about your choices. Put the call out to the grandparents, aunties, and uncles to bring you a framed picture for your wall of portraits. (They should be highly motivated when you tell them it's for baby to get to know them better.)

If your family can't be trusted to select tasteful frames, take your baby along to a frame store and choose the type you like best. Or check out the Picturewall Company on the Web, which supplies everything you need to make this project as easy as possible. Once your wall of fame is in place, walk by with your baby, point out each person, and say their names aloud.

#176 Eat your own dog food.

For those of you not in the business world, the expression "eat your own dog food" means that you should be willing to use the product you're selling. As in, "I'm not just the president of the Hair Club for Men; I'm also a member." Or, in this case: Take your own advice.

We frequently call each other and say, "What should I do this afternoon?" What?! We, the authors of hundreds of activities, cannot think of anything to do today? "We should eat our own dog food," Heather might say, meaning that we should check the posts on our very own Web site for an idea we haven't tried recently.

Do you find that you're a genius when giving other people care, compassion, and good advice, but you're not so good at taking it? Your challenge for today is to do an activity you have recommended to someone else.

#177 *Drive and listen.*

If your baby's nap is dependent on your taking her for a car ride, you might want to consider some entertainment onboard your daily drives. If you're low tech, try some audio books. If you're high tech, try podcasts. Listen and learn. Plus then you'll have something more compelling to discuss than poop or sleep!

The iTunes store has many audiobooks and podcasts to browse. Check out Audible.com for other options. Important note: If you're planning to listen to your MP3 player in the car, invest in the little gadget that lets you listen through your car's speakers. Please, for everyone's safety, do not be a jackass in headphones. Heather thanks you.

#178 *Surprise your partner with a night out.*

You plan it.

You secure the babysitter.

You pick up the check.

You spend the rest of the week reminding him how awesome you are.

#179 *Fake 'em out.*

Save your old sunglasses, cell phones, remotes, and key chains in a drawer, then pull them out one at a time as a good rainy-day baby activity. While she plays with one item, you can usually sneak another into the drawer and reintroduce it later for an endless supply of playthings.

Sometimes when Whitney really needs to remove her cell phone from Julian's little paws, a decoy cell phone is the best way to avoid a minitantrum.

#180 *Help your baby be reflective.*

Babies are self-centered little buggers! They think we're just an extension of them, and we know from experience that we're just here to service their every whim.

Record your baby's egomania on film by taking this frame-worthy picture. Strip your baby down to a diaper and position her in front of a mirror. Take her picture from behind so that you capture both her back and her front, as reflected in the mirror. Before taking the photo, open all the window coverings to fill the room with natural light. Avoid using a flash—you don't want to see it in the mirror.

#181 *Finger paint.*

We certainly did not appreciate the preciousness of little handprints until we had our own offspring's tiny hands to adore, so reserve this potentially cheesy project for a grandparent gift.

To make personalized wrapping paper or note cards, dip your baby's hand into finger paint or press it on a nontoxic inkpad intended for stamping. Then help your baby make handprints on blank cards or wrapping paper. You can buy plain butcher paper to use as wrapping paper or just use the wrong side (the white side) of wrapping paper you already have.

Overachiever Option: Make first-birthday party invitations using your baby's handprint.

Geeky Option: Photograph or scan the handprints so you can use them for future projects.

#182 Slide on the playground.

Are you ready to see some big smiles? Or looks of horror? Be prepared for either.

Whitney's nanny taught her the following method for putting Julian on the slide when he was too young to slide sitting up. This activity is pretty safe. (But please note: We are not doctors or paramedics, so proceed at your own risk.) After you get comfortable with it, you can let go and let her slide by herself.

1 Put baby on her tummy, feet down, midway on the slide.

2 Put her hands near her face, not down at her sides. Hopefully she is holding her head up so that you don't smear her face against the metal as she goes down.

3 Let her slide down to the bottom.

4 Repeat. Repeat. Repeat. Then sit down and let baby play in the sand while you think about that spa you're never going to visit.

#183 *Make dinner after dinner.*

After you finish cleaning up the dishes from tonight's dinner and baby is down for the night, crack open a bottle of wine with your partner and work on tomorrow's meal.

Cooking without urgency or starvation (and a small amount of inebriation) is actually pleasant. Reconnect over chopping and rinsing while doing the kitchen tango for counter space and sink time. The extra bonus is that tomorrow's food will be ready when you want to eat it. Heather and her husband make dinner for the next day as their evening bonding activity. At first, they did this by mistake, like when they thought beef stew or lasagna was something they could just throw together in an hour and had to eat something (like the old standby, cold cereal) while cooking.

#184 *Host a play date.*

At this age, play dates are pretty much for you rather than the baby. If your child is on a wacky nap schedule, or if leaving the house is a big pain, offer to host a playdate at your place so that your pals and their little ones can come to you. That way your baby can wake up when she pleases and join the fun at her convenience, and you might even get the chance to have a conversation with your guests.

Provide a few clean blankets, some toys, and munchies for the parents.

#185 *Host a TV night with your pals.*

By 8 or 9 months, the typical baby is asleep for a solid stretch between 8 P.M. and midnight—and who can say what she's got planned for you after that. But mamas, we cannot sit around every night watching TV alone, waiting for little peeps from the baby monitor. To change up your situation, invite some friends over to watch TV with you. It's nighttime socializing, with no babysitter required!

Pick a weekly show, preferably a guilty pleasure, and invite your childfree girlfriends or couple-friends to join you on a regular basis. Alternate who provides dinner (take-out is encouraged, of course) and make sure your TV is set to record the show in case you have to duck out during a juicy part to take care of a fussy baby.

Set the bar high at your inaugural TV night by providing food, dessert, and a game to go along with the show (think trivia, drinking games, drawing contest). That'll ensure your friends will want to come back next week.

#186 Resell some mini clothes.

Purge your little buddha's closet. Be ruthless about it. Keeping baby clothes you don't like is just adding clutter to your life. And if you sell your least favorites at a used clothing store, you can use the credit immediately to buy things you do like.

While you're at it, review the too-small clothes you were thinking of storing. Consider each item and ask yourself if you would actually put it on a second child. If not, why keep it?

Haul yourselves over to a secondhand kid's store and trade in your cast-offs. The most lucrative resales are name-brand, new-looking items with the tags still attached. From now on, when gifts of clothing are just too ugly for words and aren't from a store you know, take them in immediately for resale. Even if you get only $3 for a pair of orange plaid overalls and matching sweater, wouldn't you rather have a vanilla latte than look at them again?

Note: Repeat every 6 months.

#187 *Leave the house no matter what.*

Rainy? Snowy? Go to the mall.

#188 *Throw an Inside-Outside party.*

Your baby has now been on the outside longer than she was on the inside, so it's time to celebrate!

Unless you're currently knocked up, we suggest doing all those things you weren't allowed to do (in good conscience, anyway) while you were pregnant. Stuff like:

> ★ **Drink wine** ★ **Eat soft imported cheese** ★ **Luxuriate in a hot tub**
> ★ **Ride an ostrich or mechanical bull** ★ **Bungee jump from a bridge**

If your favorite indulgence is not on this list, go ahead and improvise. It kind of makes you wonder, though—if these things are so bad for the pregnants, why do we allow ourselves these dangers at all?

#189 Go to bed early, but not to sleep (wink, wink).

Since you won't find either of us jumping up from our late-evening half-asleep position on the couch to initiate some hot action in the bedroom, we'll assume the same goes for you. Volunteer to make it worth your honey's while if he'll go to bed early with you.

#190 Feed your kid on the floor.

Dads sometimes have a different approach to problem solving than moms, and it's often more direct. Whitney's husband suggests that since your baby doesn't really care what high chair you carefully selected for her—and she will toss her food willynilly over the tray regardless—you should ditch the chair once in a while and serve a meal on the floor. That's where the food's headed anyway.

Now We're Cruising

MONTHS 10 THROUGH 12

Can you believe your rookie year is coming to a close? Just a few looks back to your baby's newborn pictures will have you shaking your head in disbelief. You're getting used to the idea that you're the mom, right? Whether you're hyper-organized, laid-back, or just goofy, new moms with younger babies are looking at you and thinking that you have it figured out. You look like the "real mom" now. Excellent progress, mama.

.... YOUR NEW SKILLS ....

- ★ Understanding baby's grunts and gestures
- ★ Rediscovering your inner child
- ★ Dodging flying finger foods
- ★ Enjoying yourself in the evenings
- ★ Thinking about topics other than babies

.... YOUR NEW FEARS ....

- ★ You'll never be able to balance career, love, and family
- ★ You can't connect with your childless friends as often or as easily
- ★ You have to get dinner on the table every freaking night
- ★ You'll never find enough time for everyone — especially yourself

For years, people have maintained a healthy marriage and raised a child. In fact, many of them start working on another baby around the end of this first year. As your pre-baby self becomes more of a distant memory, you should be able to take advantage of our evening entertainment ideas and find more opportunities to bond with your partner. Whatever your comfort level, we've got suggestions for both family-friendly outings and creative dates. We're here to warn you: You better start cruising now, because toddlerhood offers no rest for the weary.

Month

10

#191 *Meet your friends for errands.*

It used to be that running out to the drugstore or grocery store was a non-event. Well, not anymore. We invite you to think of these routine errands as miniadventures and an opportunity to be semi-social. It's a total win-win — you can bring your baby, meet some friends, and Get Things Done all at the same time. Many times, we meet with the kids to do some shopping and ask ourselves if it counts as a developmentally appropriate outing. The answer is "yes."

Wander the aisles of your most colorful grocery store with a buddy you haven't seen for a while. Dole out Cheerios or veggie puffs to keep your little one in good spirits while you fill up your cart. Plan your cart-filling well, though, because once ice cream is in the mix, your outing is about to end. The goal is to get out of there before either your baby or your frozen goods have a meltdown.

#192 *Attend bookstore events.*

Big chains and independent bookstores alike offer story times for babies and children. Research these opportunities to let someone else entertain your baby.

What to expect: You'll sit and listen to a story with the baby on your lap. It may include some songs or finger play. The end.

These events are short, so don't be late!

Related activity: #109, Check out the library, page 95

#193 Pack a sack of surprises.

While your baby is sleeping, pack a bunch of toys in a duffle bag for him to dis-cover and pull out of the bag when he wakes up. Whitney's son always unpacked everything to the right, so if she acted quickly enough, she could keep refilling the bag from the left.

You might also consider simply packing up toys to store them; you can rotate sets of toys by swapping the bags every now and then.

#194 Play hooky from work.

If you're a working mom, you probably feel like you're missing out when you read about things like drop-in music classes or 10 A.M. coffee dates with friends. Call in sick one day (blame it on a sick baby) and do all the fun things you think stay-at-home moms are doing.

If you're a stay-at-home mom, share this idea with your partner. Encourage him to play hooky from work one day to go to a baby-and-me class while you get your own day off!

#195 Host a board-game night.

Are you a Trivial Pursuit purist, Cranium geek, or Scrabble addict? Game night is an easy way to entertain a group of friends on the cheap once baby is in bed for the night. Supply snacks or desserts and drinks, and ask your buddies to bring their favorite games. Let the crowd decide what looks like the most fun, and let the games begin!

#196 Help a rookie mom.

Hey, you weren't even paying attention and suddenly you're an old-pro of a new mom. You can operate your stroller, identify your baby's sleepy signs, and feed him applesauce while talking on your cell phone.

Do you know anyone with a baby younger than yours? If so, be a sweetie and:

- ★ Help her in or out of a doorway.
- ★ Make her a meal and bring it over.
- ★ Take her baby for a quick walk so she can nap.
- ★ Chaperone her on an easy outing, on her schedule.
- ★ Buy her a copy of this book, with some of your favorite activities marked.

#197 *Test-drive some music classes.*

Most music classes for children provide a free trial session. Scan the Web sites of music schools in your area to find out the details, and take advantage of the freebies before committing to paying the fee.

HERE ARE TWO ORGANIZATIONS
.... **THAT OFFER CLASSES WORLDWIDE** ....

★ **Kindermusik Village** (www.kindermusik.com) classes are for babies younger than 18 months. Each class lasts 45 minutes.
★ **Music Together** (www.musictogether.com) offers mixed-age classes through age 5. Classes are an hour long.

#198 *Escape solo.*

Talk to your mate to establish a plan for each of you to experience some solitude. Take turns leaving the house alone for free time during baby naptime or for a longer block of time on a weekend. Jump on your bike and take a slow, quiet ride. Walk through a department store and leisurely try on clothes. Hit a nearby café on your own and read like you don't have a care in the world. Decadence.

#199 *Make a memory game.*

Here's a gift idea: Make a personalized version of the game Memory. You know, where you turn over two tiles to try to make a match. Each time you find a match, you remove the tiles until you've matched all the pairs. In your personalized version, the pictures on the tiles are your family members. You can even borrow our own cute title, Family Memory. Present the box to the grandparents, and you will be the most-admired gift giver at your gathering.

Here's how:

1 **Visit the craft store** and purchase 16 wood blocks and a tray or gift box in which to store them.

2 **Choose 8 photos of family members,** either alone or in pairs. Crop and resize each until it's the same size as the surface of the blocks. If you're using digital photos and aren't proficient in a graphics program, you can do this task in Microsoft Word. Just paste the image into a document and use the tools in the Picture toolbar to alter it.

3 **Print two copies of each** adjusted photo on photo paper.

4 **Cut out the images and use clear glue to adhere them to the blocks.** Seal them with a coat of shellac or shiny, protective spray.

5 **Type up instructions for playing the game,** just to make the gift a little sweeter.

#200 *Give your baby a pickle.*

What?! Yep, a pickle spear for a baby. This little trick was discovered by Heather as she tried to juggle both baby and a slice of pizza. Well, he loved his pickle, and it kept his mitts off her lunch!

Informal polling of other rookie moms proved that 3 out of 4 also gave their toothless kids pickles to make 'em happy.

Stick a pickle spear in that greedy hand. Just watch closely to make sure your little piglet doesn't gnaw off any chunks. This activity loses its charm when baby starts to choke.

#201 Contain yourself, baby.

Having extra laundry baskets around is critical. Now that you have a child, these handy containers have gained a few new responsibilities.

1 **Free babysitter.** Sometimes Heather just puts Holden in a basket to keep him contained while she does something nearby (like pack a suitcase or empty the dryer). When he gets antsy, she hands him different objects to examine.

2 **Home base for the unfold-erator.** You can painstakingly fold laundry, and your baby can pull it right back out of the basket. Great game, right? Let us assure you that at around 12 months, he will begin putting the laundry back into the basket; actually refolding it will take a few more years.

3 **Transportation provider.** The train game is 3 easy steps to rainy-day fun. You can drive the laundry-land express around in a circle or through your entire house. Just pad the sides and bottom of a clothesbasket with pillows or laundry, put the baby inside, and push him around like a train. All aboard!

#202 *Have a ball.*

If you still have a yoga ball (even if you're not currently using it for ab work), get it out to thrill and delight your baby. Try one of our rookie mom–tested ideas or come up with more of your own.

.... **THIS IS HOW THESE BABIES ROLL** ....

* **Pepper likes surfing around on her tummy on top of the ball.** Her mom, Jeanine, supplies the balance.
* **Holden really likes to sit next to the ball and push it.** When it hits the wall and then rolls back, he is amazed.
* **Julian loves standing next to the ball while Whitney dribbles it** by smacking her hands on top of it.

#203 *Find some excellent graffiti.*

This adventure is for all the urban mamas. It's time for a scavenger hunt! Take a picture of your baby in front of graffiti. The gritty background serves as an excellent contrast to the sweetness that is your baby, and scoping out the locations is a fun way to incorporate your former, edgier self into your parenting.

#204 *Make a gift for less than $10 in less than 10 minutes.*

Looking for a cheap gift for a baby or toddler? A "treasure box" is a great present for pretty much any kid, even babies.

To make one, buy a gift box, a plastic container with dividers, or one of those cute faux-vintage lunchboxes. Then purchase a pack of alphabet stickers, available at large discount stores or craft stores.

Use them to put the recipient's name on the box. We like to add "Treasures," as in "Milo's Treasures," but if the child's name has too many S's or E's, you might not have enough letters.

Depending on your budget, put some treats in the box or just leave it empty. For an older baby, we suggest small plastic animals or bath toys. For a big girl, provide crayons and stickers. For your 24-year-old sister, leave the box empty so she can put her souvenirs from Italy inside.

#205 *Ride a real bus or train.*

Give your baby a thrill and take a trip on a public bus, train, or trolley. Rookie mom Becky reported, "My son loves trains, and for him, riding the T [in Boston] is a special treat. When Nick was a newborn, we just took him on the train in the Björn."

If your baby requires a stroller, bring a small, collapsible one to avoid the extra bulk (and the wrath of other passengers).

#206 *Turn on your blender and get salty.*

Invite some friends over on a warm day for a Margarita Mommies Group. If you do this activity correctly, the babies will be having so much fun slurping on plastic toys and touching one another's toes that they won't realize their moms are having fun, too.

.... **INGREDIENTS FOR A SUCCESSFUL FIESTA** ....

- ★ **Shady backyard** on a nice, summery day.
- ★ **Kiddie pool** filled with a couple of inches of water.
- ★ **Mom-sized lawn chairs** placed close enough to the pool for dipping toes in the water.
- ★ **Plastic cups and pitcher brimming with margaritas.**
- ★ **Splashing babies** (diapers optional). Keep them in the shade and slather them heavily with sunscreen before the party starts!
- ★ **Daddies available to pick up mommy and baby when the party's over.**

#207 *Use TV as a tool.*

Both of us tend to be firm on the topic of "no TV" for the babies, and each for her own reasons. Heather thinks that TV is a scary addiction for babies, not unlike crack. Whitney fears TV addiction actually threatens parents, not babies, as it sure is tempting to have your baby in a glazed-over state of relaxation. And, oh yeah, we read that watching television isn't recommended by the American Academy of Pediatrics for children under 2.

If you already use TV as a babysitter, then you're probably smarter than we are. Plus your kid will probably turn out smarter than ours, too, logging in all those hours of *Sesame Street* before preschool even starts. But if you are TV-shy, consider leveraging its magical powers from time to time to accomplish the following:

* **Cut your child's nails** while he's distracted by children's programming.
* **Trim his hair** while he sits in the high chair in front of the TV.
* **Pass time on a long trip** by turning on a portable DVD player.
* **Face the high chair toward the TV at a pub** and enjoy your friends and a little beer while baby watches "the game."

#208 Get hands-on and learn something.

Most cities have a science museum, and kids under 2 are usually admitted for free.
Pay a visit to one of these museums. Explore the exhibits and narrate for your
baby. Anything with water or lights will pique his interest.

Both you and your child will be fascinated by the older kids—and how
their parents struggle to wrangle these bipedal creatures.

#209 *Do what YOU want to do.*

Think about one thing you would do if it were just you, on your own. Or something you'd do if you were hosting an old friend you rarely see and want to impress. Would you visit a museum showing an important art exhibition? Take a drive to a beautiful place and go for a hike just to see the view? Or would you hit an urban café and chat with strangers at nearby tables, just to feel the buzz of the city?

Dive in and do that thing with your baby, even if it seems like it might be stressful. We promise, it won't be half as bad as you fear. It might even be great. If it helps, consider this activity as an opportunity to create a special date with your baby. You may end up having a truly memorable experience.

#210 *Treat yourself to a quickie meal.*

If your partner is out of town or working late, getting yourself a fast, cheap dinner has definite appeal. Wouldn't you rather throw away a paper bag after eating than scrape and wash dishes?

Fast-food chains are filled with noisy big kids, which offers two key benefits: Your tot is not the loudest one in the joint, and he'll have plenty of people to look at. Give yourself permission for a guilty-pleasure meal and pull up a stroller or high chair.

Month

11

#211 *Take 1-2-3 pictures.*

You know those picture frames with 3 spaces in them? They're not just for people with 3 children. They're for you.

Fill one up with photos that work well together. Get to know the settings on your digital camera—most will allow you to take a series of quick photos. Use this feature to capture your baby's ability to clap or wave. Or document all the expressions that lead up to a smile or the progress of sweet potato from spoon to face to hair.

Then frame 3 photos together to show the action. So cute, right?

#212 *Document baby's birthplace.*

Take a picture of your baby that captures the essence of the city or town in which she was born. Palm trees, skyscrapers, big red barns—what typifies your location? Your photo may have a famous landmark in the background, or maybe you'll prop baby on the shoulders of a local celebrity. Both our boys have had their pictures taken in front of the Golden Gate Bridge. If you have several ideas, explore them all!

Tonight, show your partner the postcard-worthy results of your photo shoot.

#213 *Hit on another baby owner.*

Think you're too shy to just start talking to a new and possibly interesting person? Your baby is a great social lubricant, you know. Today's assignment is to approach someone else who has a baby. Check out the other duo and prepare your "pick-up line." Then go for it.

.... **HERE ARE SOME SUGGESTIONS TO BREAK THE ICE** ....

★ **"Where did you find that toy?"**
★ **"How do you like that stroller/diaper bag?"**
★ **"I love your _____."**
★ **"How old is s/he?"**
★ Or the old standby, **"What a nice day for _____ [what you're doing]."**

#214 *Host a wine-tasting fete.*

This is a fun activity to follow all the *Goodnight Moon* or *You Are My Sunshine* your early-evening routine requires. Ask your buddies to come about a half hour after your bedtime routine usually wraps up, so you can stay nice and relaxed. Buy a couple bottles of wine of the same varietal (make it a Pinot party!). Hide the labels with paper bags or homemade labels and mark the bottles "A," "B," "C," or "D," so you can tell them apart. Hand out scorecards, with a line for each wine, A through D. Then taste each one, rate it, tally the score, and declare a winner.

Serve the winning wine at the next easy dinner party you throw (see page 142) or give a bottle to the friend with the most creative wine descriptions. (Something like "I taste Asian flowers with a hint of vine, finished by a dirty oak barrel" might take the prize at one of our parties.)

For other suggestions for fun evenings at home, see activity #185 on page 156 and activity #195 on page 166.

#215 *Disco in your living room.*

Invite some of your mommy pals over for a rockin' playdate. Dim the lights, put on some fun music, and bop around the living room with a roomful of creepers and cruisers.

Shake it until naptime.

#216 Visit a farm.

Take a day trip to see live animals. You probably don't have to go too far from home to find a petting zoo or a working farm with a few goats and sheep.

To cement a solid four-legged friendship, bring lettuce or celery along to feed the animals.

#217 *Find your snow-day destinations.*

Before the weather gets nasty, figure out where your boisterous almost-toddler can blow off steam. Places like kids' museums, play cafés, and the library are obvious choices, but consider variations on the theme, like the pet store, bookstores, big box stores, and the mall.

Make a list of your favorites so that when the rains pour down or the snow piles up, you'll remember your options.

#218 *Have a crawling race.*

OK, you might feel like a total idiot, but some days we find ourselves housebound and we have to be creative.

The funniest thing about this game is that your baby doesn't really know she's racing you. To heat things up, you need to quickly crawl up to her (in the same direction she's already crawling) and then challenge her to a race by crawling faster and making noise to show you're excited—much as a person at a stoplight might start revving the engine to challenge you to a drag race.

#219 Pack a picnic.

We like to keep our picnics simple. Ideally, cleanup should require just a vigorous shake of the blanket into the grass, leaving the Cheerio crumbs to the bugs. Here's how to have your own carefree picnic lunch:

1 **Pack the requisite gear while baby is napping.**
2 **Pick up your lunch at a favorite deli or take-out joint.** In other words, don't hurt yourself by cooking if you don't have to.
3 **Head to the local park or favorite grassy patch,** blanket in tow.
4 **Enjoy the first-rate free entertainment of just sitting there.** Other fun may include watching other kids, dogs, caterpillars, and bugs; touching cold, prickly grass; and dancing through the leaves.

#220 Go on an anti-shopping trip.

Visit a large toy store and let baby try out all the things you aren't going to buy. Wouldn't it be great if you could teach your child that toy stores are places we can go to enjoy toys without necessarily bringing any home?

#221 Craft a bulletin board.

By hanging a bulletin board on your child's wall, you enable an ever-changing assortment of things to look at, images that reflect her true personality rather than the babyish decor you chose before you even met her. By now your baby probably has some interests or hobbies, such as dogs, the moon, or eating. Give her a place to display pictures and mementos she'll enjoy reviewing before bed each night.

1 **Purchase a plain cork bulletin board.** Paint the frame if you want to.

2 **Buy a couple yards of fabric.** Use this opportunity to buy fabric you love but haven't otherwise had an excuse to purchase.

3 **Staple the fabric over the corky bits.**

4 **If you're feeling fancy, pin a grid of ribbons across the surface.** Then you can easily tuck cards into it when the mood strikes you.

5 **Hang the bulletin board** prominently inside or outside the baby's room.

#222 Go on a rustic hike.

Sick of strolling on the sidewalks? Find a woodsy nature trail and take a rustic hike. Feed your wobbler dry cereal and pretend it's trail mix, or pack a picnic lunch for yourself and some friends.

#223 *Get all sexy.*

Forgive us if we sound like a housewife's guide straight out of the 1950s, but we're gonna suggest that you fix yourself up a little more for excursions with your mate. Are you still wearing your playground shoes? Is your shirt stained with pureed carrots or peas? Is your hair in the same ponytail from this morning? Snap out of it.

Find a flattering outfit and put on a little makeup for your next evening out (or in). Meow.

#224 *Record baby laughing or babbling.*

This time next year, your baby will be speaking in sentences! They may be short ones, like "bird fly high," or long ones, like "garbage truck take dirty diapers away," but it's gonna happen before you know it.

Use your digital camera to capture some of the preverbal grunts, babbles, or (if you can make it happen) a full-on laugh. Your future preschooler will be so amused to hear herself this way.

#225 Let your baby use the phone.

"Oh my gosh, I'm so sorry, my baby just called you." Don't you wish you had that excuse in college when you were drunk-dialing your ex-boyfriend? Now you do!

You know it's going to happen sooner or later, so give your baby a thrill and hand over the phone. As long as she doesn't press 9-1-1, it's all good, and you never know just who you'll end up reconnecting with.

While she's distracted by the phone, you can focus on something you want to do, like setting up TiVo. To get the phone away from baby, you may need to be ready to trade the remote.

#226 Join Crawlers Anonymous.

Once the bambino is crawling, you're pretty much kicked out of postpartum yoga. Consider an activity like Gymboree, a music and movement class for babies of all ages. Look for a free trial class to see if you like it. Many gymnastics studios also have Mommy and Me classes, often with a free introductory class if you remember to ask for it.

Children's museums are also great places to explore, and most offer annual memberships. Many have special infant and toddler areas that feature soft, crawler-friendly structures and age-appropriate "exhibits." Go with a friend and ask for a tour to see if your kid is ready for it. If you have out-of-town family, this type of membership can do double duty when you visit them because many institutions have reciprocal agreements.

The benefit of baby gyms and children's museums is that you can drop in when it's convenient for you rather than getting to a class at a specified time. This is especially appealing for rainy days when the living room is getting tiresome.

#227 *Photograph the inanimate objects, too.*

If your baby has a security object, such as a blanket or stuffed animal, take a photo of it, too. The much-loved item will get increasingly ragged over time, and it'll be nice to remember what its original shape was.

HOW TO CAPTURE THE OBJECT
.... **OF YOUR CHILD'S AFFECTION** ....

★ **For the sentimental:** Sneak into her bedroom and take a photo of her snuggling up to Lovey while she sleeps.

★ **For the artsy:** Take a roll of wrapping paper that's white on one side. Unroll a fair amount and drape it from the coffee table onto the ground. Position Lovey on the paper and get down on the ground to shoot the photo. You might need to use the "macro" setting (usually represented by a flower icon on a digital camera) to get a clear close-up.

★ **For the absurdist:** Photograph Lovey outside, on the grass, on a lounge chair, or hanging in a tree.

★ **For the bad girl:** Position Lovey doing adult activities, such as drinking beer, watching TV, or driving the car.

#228 Run (or walk) errands.

If you're reading this book looking for a suggestion you can act on today, this is it: Run errands. For real, girls, run them. Or walk, if you're not a runner. Do as many errands as you can on foot.

Put the kid in the stroller or backpack and head out the door to the place you need to go. If it's within 2 miles, this feat is reasonable. If you live up in the hills or out in the burbs, you can drive to a closer location and start from there. For many of us, however, we'd guess that food and necessities are findable within 2 miles from home. You can do it!

#229 Go dog watching.

If your kid is not yet saying "doggie," well, what's wrong with you? Seek out a dog park for an outing. Even if you have a dog at home, your little guy will enjoy seeing all the shapes and sizes they come in. If you're scared of dogs, stand outside the fenced area and look in.

P.S. We'll be honest: at the age of 1 year, neither of our babies was anywhere near saying "doggie."

#230 *Produce a year-end DVD.*

We know, we know. You have a bunch of video footage of baby and you don't know how to access it, download it, or upload it, much less how to add subtitles and music. You are not alone.

Instead of tearing your hair out over this project, we recommend you choose one of the following strategies, neither of which involves doing it yourself.

1   **Outsource.** Pay someone. Hand over all your discs, tapes, or memory cards and let them have at it. This is costly but labor-free for you.

2   **Delegate.** Recruit your partner to be accountable for the project's outcome. You gave birth, so he owes you, right?

If you're one of those unique parents who actually knows how to maneuver all the video clips, take a few hours and string together about 20 minutes' worth of the highlights. This video is guaranteed to be one of your future toddler's favorites.

Month

12

#231 Meow, bark, and tweet at the pet store.

We've found that a super-sized pet store is a stimulating destination for soon-to-be 1-year-olds. At this age, visiting a pet store is actually better than the zoo, and the parking is easier, too. The animals are displayed in eye-level cages and tanks, so you and baby can easily peer into them together. You can get up-close and personal with screeching birds, slimy frogs, and furry rodents.

Since you can pop in for a minute or two, the pet store is ideal for filling time right before a meal or nap.

Is your pet store situated among other errand-running destinations? Drop your partner and baby there while you run off to accomplish other chores, such as shoe shopping. And to kill two birds with one stone (no offense, bird lovers), you could be really nice and pick up pet food for a postpartum friend while entertaining your own baby with a free, super-fun outing.

#232 *Throw a backyard festival.*

Entertaining your wobbler is best done outside, when possible. Give yourself a break by setting up several play stations at once, so your little guy can roam from activity to activity while you sit back and stare into space. To make it more fun and even easier to clean up, invite friends with babies to come by and contribute.

············ **IDEAS FOR BACKYARD STATIONS** ············

★ **Water.** You'll be shocked by how long an 11-month-old will remain entertained in front of a large plastic bowl of water and some measuring cups or spoons.

★ **Tunnel.** Collapsible nylon tunnels can be inexpensively at toy stores. They're also good indoors during those long winter months.

★ **Kiddie pool.** Inflate the pool, fill it with 2–3 inches (5–7.5 cm) of water, and set the babies inside. Show them how to dip plastic toys in it, or just let them lean over and splash. Make sure you watch them carefully.

★ **Bubbles.** This one requires some actual effort on your part. If you're truly lazy, buy an automatic bubble blower.

★ **Minitent.** Set up a special baby tent specifically for backyard escapades. Or consider putting up your real tent for a few weeks of summer fun.

★ **Push toys.** Durable little ride-around cars are super fun.

★ **Balls.** Simple inflatable balls are awesome for babies and toddlers. And they're cheap, too.

#233 Print baby trading cards.

If you have a critical mass of munchkins showing up at a first-birthday party or play group, make baby trading cards to hand out as favors.

.... **WHAT YOU NEED** ....

★ **Current pictures and stats:** Ask the moms to e-mail a photo of their child and a few trivia facts.

★ **Trading cards:** Purchase business cards that can be loaded into an ink-jet printer. Sheets usually contain 8 cards.

★ **A computer with word-processing program.**

.... **HOW TO MAKE THEM** ....

1 Use the word-processing template that goes with your printable business cards. The template number will be printed on the card package.

2 Input text and images into each card space.

3 Print a full set for each family at your party.

4 Shuffle all the cards so they're not in order.

.... **AT THE PARTY** ....

Give each family the number of cards that are in a full set. Some will get doubles or triples of one baby and none of another. Tell guests to begin trading to make a complete set, one of each baby. At our party, we had parents walking around saying, "I have two Theos. I need an Ava. Who has an Ava?"

#234 Stay out 'til dark.

The challenge is to take the kid, hit the road with another mom friend, and stay out of the house until bedtime.

One day, we put both of our car seats into one vehicle* and packed in the boys, armed with their snacks and sippy cups. Then we set out to do some random silly activities. And we took lots of pictures. For our awfully big adventure, we:

* **Put babies in photo booth** and struggled to keep both in the frame.
* **Crawled around an unfamiliar mall's play zone.**
* **Got free professional photos taken.**
* **Rented bumper-car-style strollers.**

You could go see some trains, explore a new mall, find an aquarium, or head to a nearby suburb to explore their toddler attractions.

Part of the adventure is discovering what you forgot to bring and then making a scavenger hunt out of finding a solution. In our excitement over being in one car together, we both forgot to bring our strollers, so we rented them at a mall. Yes, we felt like superfreaks with bumper-car-shaped strollers for 1-year-olds, but the boys were happy.

* The first time you try this activity, allow yourself a half hour to deal with car-seat adjustments. The second time we did it, it took less than 10 minutes.

#235 *Share a milkshake.*

There are a couple things about milkshakes that small people really like. Drinking with a straw is one of them. Watching Mommy make it is the other. There are a couple things moms like about milkshakes, too. One is the opportunity to feed their young cubs both milk and the magic superfood blueberries at the same time. Another is that none of it—well, *less* of it—ends up on the floor because baby is so captivated by the whole straw experience.

The key to an easy, quick smoothie is a stick mixer, also known as an immersion blender. This tool is helpful for all baby-food making. There's no setup and, when you're done, it takes 2 seconds to clean.

.... **HOW TO MAKE THE SHAKE** ....

Put about 10 frozen blueberries, 1 cup (240 ml) of milk, a handful of strawberries, and a banana into a plastic container. Insert mixer and blend. Pour into a plastic cup and add a straw. Add a second straw for extra fun.

#236 Document the latest obsession.

We've noticed that kids love repetition, redundancy, and repetitiveness.

Are you confident that your baby will point to the fan and grunt enthusiastically every. single. morning when you bring him into the bedroom? Does he yell "puh-puh!" with the same level of unbridled enthusiasm each time a puppy dog walks by? These are the behaviors that distinguish our child's unique personality.

Don't let your baby's obsessive habits go undocumented. Try to capture them with a photograph or video. Take notes and stick them in an album somewhere. It won't be long before he drops one wacky habit in favor of a new one.

#237 Wish for nonmaterial gifts.

Your home is probably already packed with clutter, so allow us to suggest a few first-birthday gifts that will not result in more stuff to put away, step around, or sterilize. Pass these along to your parents when they ask what to buy your munchkin for his big day.

* ★ Membership to a museum or zoo
* ★ Music classes
* ★ Babysitting hours or payment of the babysitter
* ★ Gift certificate for shoes for your wobbly new walker

#238 Pitch a tent at an outdoor store.

There's tons of fun to be had with baby at camping- and hiking-supply stores. Set up a cozy hideaway in a display tent with several camping mattresses, chirping bird toys, and brightly colored water bottles. Have a blast.

Even if the tent doesn't work out, this outing can also be fun for tiny tentative toddlers who just want to follow the path around the store endlessly.

But a word of caution: The first time Heather did this activity with Holden, he was most interested in chewing tags off the merchandise, so watch out for that!

#239 For a good time, check the garage.

Do you have gear you never use? Pull out your backpack or jogging stroller, even if you just go for a walk around the block. Your kid will be intrigued by the new device.

Other treats you might find in the garage: a baby bathtub might be good for water play, infant toys can be rediscovered and appreciated once again, and sports equipment or camping supplies may reveal fun objects to be explored or dragged around the living room for a few hours.

#240 *Use your clutter to entertain your baby.*

This one's especially good if you feel like your living room is already an obstacle course. Now you can refer to it as a developmentally appropriate baby gymnasium!

Set up some roadblocks so that baby can test his mobility skills. Try a couple pillows, some toys, a plastic bowl, and even some magazines. Then let the crawling, rolling, and lurching begin. Watch your baby navigate the challenges of a new situation. Help him out if you're so inclined.

#241 *Play the shell game.*

To prepare your baby for the fact that life is hard and that he may eventually be earning his living playing con games against tourists on the streets of New York City, you'll want to introduce him to the shell game.

Take 3 plastic cups or bowls and put them facedown on the ground after first showing him which one his Cheerio is underneath. Swap the positions of the cups and then let baby flip one over.

We use cups that are somewhat see-through, so it's not really testing the baby's sense of object permanence. But it is fun to see him make a choice and pick up one of the cups.

#242 *Get more out of* Goodnight Moon.

Whitney will readily admit that when she first added *Goodnight Moon* to Julian's bedtime ritual, she found the book sort of boring. Then, after a few months, she found the book *painfully* boring.

One day, our friend Sunny said, "I see new things in that book every time I look at it." Really?! We started paying more attention and found things we'd never noticed before. If you're in the same boat, scrutinize the illustrations in the other books you read to your baby. You might develop new favorites.

5 OBSERVATIONS TO HEIGHTEN
YOUR INTEREST IN *GOODNIGHT MOON*

★ **The bunny is in a different position** in bed each time the bed is pictured.

★ **The time on the clocks advances** as the moon's position changes.

★ **The mouse is in a different location** on each page.

★ **The light and dark areas of the pages vary.** The reader's eye is being drawn somewhere new on each page.

★ **Is this a living room or a bedroom?** A studio apartment? Where's the kitchen? Who made that mush? Think about it.

#243 *Try out a trailer.*

Those pull-along bike trailers are cool, right? Our friend Erin has one that's made to carry both her kids. So much fun! When Erin had only one bambino, she used the extra space for Target purchases.

Yes, my friend, you can ride your bike to Target, with baby tucked in the trailer, and shop your little head off. Isn't life grand?

One time, Erin and Whitney rode their bikes to a breakfast spot, carting both of their 11-month-olds in Erin's trailer. Julian fell asleep with his big helmet head smushing Erin's son's face.

If you know you wouldn't do this activity often enough to justify the purchase of your own bike trailer, call around to find out if you can rent a bike with a child seat or trailer already attached and take a special outing. Don't forget to ask for a baby-sized helmet as well.

#244 *Meet a monkey at the zoo.*

It's time to introduce your little cub to lions and lizards. And won't you feel like an official parent when you brag that you take your child to The Zoo?

Truthfully, at this stage, a zoo outing is mostly fun for parents. Even at 12 months, your baby won't be able to spot many of the animals within the context of their environments. They'll probably be more excited at the sight of running water than exotic creatures.

Just like the children's museums, when you join, you get to go whenever you want for a whole year. A membership might include free parking and a few other benefits. Zoos are usually nonprofit, so membership is a feel-good thing (not to mention a tax deduction). The money helps take care of the animals. That is a good thing, since as a mother you now have a responsibility to all living things—including those nasty reptiles your child will soon be fond of.

#245 Make a fancy photo book.

If you haven't been on top of keeping a baby book, photo Web sites make it super easy to make gorgeous, coffee table–ready albums that will make you look so very organized. Consider ordering a hardcover photo book with a simple one-picture-per-month layout. If you're having fun with it, add captions, borders, and more pictures.

Alternative: If you don't feel up to the big book, a teeny mini book is great for stuffing in your purse.

#246 Keep your cool.

It's been a year, friend, and it's time to stop wearing those sweatpants so much and get your groove back. We don't care how cute or camouflaging you think they are.

Whether you were a quirky dresser with cute hair clips, the loudest girl in the bar who could entertain (or embarrass) anyone, or that savvy woman who always knew where to find the best coffee/hiking trail/vintage shoes, pick one thing to do today that will encourage you to reclaim your pre-baby personality. You might need to buy a non–parenting magazine for research, read some Web sites related to your old hobbies, or hire a babysitter to let you go wild at night.

#247 *Bring out the alpha in your baby.*

Personalized art can be expensive, and we are believers in doing it yourself. Both these DIY methods, require only a walk with your baby and a camera.

.... **INITIAL COLLAGE** ....

★ **Shoot as many items as you can that start with the first letter of your baby's name.** For example, if your baby is named Lucy, look for lights, ladders, lizards, etc.

★ **Use a photo Web site to make a collage with your best shots.** Then cut out an oversized version of your chosen letter from a piece of patterned paper and lay it on top of the collage. Frame it.

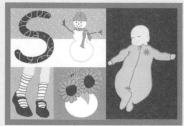

.... **ALPHABET BOOK** ....

★ **Photograph your baby next to items that begin with each letter of the alphabet, from A to Z.** Upload them to a photo Web site and order a personalized alphabet book.

#248 *Launch the first annual Camp Grandma.*

How it works: Plan an overnight trip with your partner, even if you just make reservations at a nearby hotel. Ask your baby's grandparents to come stay at your place while you're away, saving you the trouble of packing up all baby's things. Train grandma and grandpa to use the car seat, stroller, and the coffeemaker and then LET GO.

In the long run, Grandma, baby, and Mom and Dad will all look forward to this annual tradition. Since you're still a rookie, however, do this activity to the degree you feel comfortable.

Add a night to Camp Grandma each year, so that you'll take a 2-night trip around the baby's second birthday, a 3-night trip when he's 3, and so on. By the time your child is 14, dear Grandma will get 2 full weeks of adolescent merriment.

#249 *Allow baby to wear a black bean goatee.*

Black beans are healthy and fun to eat, especially when there is black bean drool rolling down your child's chin. Hey, it's probably the best entertainment you're going to get on a Friday night these days.

So find yourself a family-friendly Mexican restaurant and take your kiddo out to eat a real human meal: beans, tortilla pieces, shredded cheese, avocado.

#250 *Celebrate your way.*

You'll have plenty of chances in the years ahead to throw character-themed birthday parties, complete with goodie bags. This first big milestone is really about you. Yep, you survived that first bumpy year of parenthood—and now it's time to party!

If you're inviting others to celebrate the big O-N-E with you, make it easy on yourself by delegating food and decorations to anyone who volunteers to help.

Since your baby won't understand the event, traditional birthday-party activities are completely optional. We let our guests know that the birthday boy would not be opening gifts in front of them and that his nap began promptly at 3:30 (whether or not guests were present).

Our friend Christine honored her milestone by having dinner with her husband and hiring a babysitter. Trust us, Baby Nate had no idea he had been left out of his own birthday celebration.

Rookie Moms Milestones

When we look back in 25 years, we will marvel that our babies have become adults who drive cars and earn their own paychecks. (Here's hoping!)

You probably have a baby book to track your bambino's progress through the first year: sitting up, crawling, first tooth, and so on. But how will you remember your rookie year? After all, it's filled with important experiences that will one day make you a veteran mom, capable of coaching soccer, chaperoning school dances, and sending annoying e-mail reminders about unwritten thank-you notes.

Trust us: One day you'll look back on the early days of motherhood and it will be hard to remember them. We've given you this chart to remind you that Mommy's first full night of sleep is at least as important as baby's first banana. These classic mama milestones are worth documenting.

ROOKIE MOMS MILESTONES

First walk with baby: ★ _____ ★ _____
(Date)   (Distance/Destination)

First day spent alone with baby: ★ _____ ★ _____
(Date)   (Highlight)

First use of front carrier outside the house: ★ _____ ★ _____
(Date)   (Location)

First unpregnant cocktail: ★ _____ ★ _____
(Date)   (Drink)

First public diaper change: ★ _____ ★ _____
(Date)   (Location)

First movie with baby as date: ★ _____ ★ _____
(Movie Title)   (Date)

First day back at work: ★ _____ ★ _____
(Date)   (Highlight)

New mom friend: ★ _____ ★ _____
(Name)   (Where we met)

First road trip as a family: ★ _____ ★ _____
(Child's Name)   (Lowlight)

Least babyish hangout we frequent: ★ _____ ★ _____
(Date)   (Distance/Destination)

(Name of establishment)

ROOKIE MOMS MILESTONES

First post-baby sex: ★ _____ ★ _____
                          (Date)   (Name of partner... just kidding!)

First babysitter: ★ _____ ★ _____ ★ _____
                        (Date)   (Name)   (Where Mom was)

First time helping a rookie mom: ★ _____ ★ _____
                                       (Date)   (Favor)

First "mommy & me" class: ★ _____ ★ _____
                                (Date)   (What we learned)

First "Mom's Night Out": ★ _____ ★ _____ ★ _____
                               (Date)   (Who was there)   (Activity)

First date night: ★ _____ ★ _____
                        (Date)   (Activity)

Mom's most impressive new bra size: ★ _____
                                          (Size)

First plane trip: ★ _____ ★ _____
                        (Date)   (Distance/Destination)

First public nursing experience: ★ _____ ★ _____
                                       (Date)   (Location)

First overnight away from baby: ★ _____ ★ _____
                                      (Date)   (Distance/Destination)

209

Recommended Reading

If you can't get enough baby books, here are some Rookie Mom favorites to purchase or borrow from your local library.

- ★ **52 Projects: Random Acts of Everyday Creativity,** by Jeffrey Yamaguchi (Perigee, 2005). It's not as baby-friendly as our handy volume, but it's packed with inspiring projects and adventures to work into your day.

- ★ **Babyproofing Your Marriage: How to Laugh More, Argue Less, and Communicate Better as Your Family Grows,** by Stacie Cockrell, Cathy O'Neill, and Julia Stone (Collins, 2007). After interviewing hundreds of couples, the authors really "get it." Plus the male perspective really comes through, which can be refreshing in a sea of mommy lit.

- ★ **Confessions of a Naughty Mommy: How I Found My Lost Libido,** by Heidi Raykeil (Seal Press, 2005). Fun, quippy, and guaranteed to make you feel like less of a loser. In bed.

- ★ **Even June Cleaver Would Forget the Juice Box: Cut Yourself Some Slack (and Still Raise Great Kids) in the Age of Extreme Parenting,** by Ann Dunnewold and Sandi Kahn Shelton (HCI, 2007). This book probably speaks more to parents with older children, but we like to read ahead and be prepared.

- ★ **The Fourth Trimester: And You Thought Labor Was Hard,** by Amy Einhorn (Crown, 2001). This is a hilarious summary of the roller coaster ride we all experience during the first 6 weeks of motherhood. Whitney has read it at least 4 times.
- ★ **Get a Hobby! 101 All-Consuming Diversions for Any Lifestyle,** by Tina Barseghian (Collins, 2007). No joke, this book inspired Heather to spend a day making strawberry jam from scratch.
- ★ **The Girlfriends' Guide to Surviving the First Year of Motherhood,** by Vicki Iovine (Perigee, 1997). Practically a classic—so funny and genuinely helpful.
- ★ **Mother Shock: Loving Every (Other) Minute of It,** by Andrea J. Buchanan (Seal Press, 2003). Motherhood is compared to traveling to a foreign country where you learn the language and get acclimated. Sometimes it's total bliss, and sometimes it's embarrassingly frustrating.
- ★ **Three-Martini Family Vacation: A Field Guide to Intrepid Parenting,** by Christie Mellor (Chronicle Books, 2007). We love the author's candid way of telling us to get our ill-mannered children to behave before taking them on a fun, inexpensive holiday. Her whole philosophy is closely linked to the Rookie Moms' notion of "do what YOU want to do" (see page 176).

Index

A

alphabet book, 204
announcements, baby, 41
art, personalized, 204
audiobooks, 151

B

baby-proofing, 117
backyard festival, 193
balls, yoga, 40, 171
bathing/showering, 18, 64, 120, 132
beauty care, 43
bedroom, rearranging or redecorating, 112
bedtime routine, 75, 131
beer, 33
bike trailers, 201
birth control, 36
birth story, writing, 52
birthday celebration, first, 194, 197, 206
blankets, swaddling, 19
board books, altering, 133

bowling, 42
bras, altering, 26
breaks, scheduling, 52
breastfeeding, 19, 26, 33, 34, 67
bubbles, blowing, 148, 193
bulletin boards, decorating, 184
burp cloths, decorating, 36

C

calcium, 16
camping, 114
car-watching station, 120
car window tinting, 81
carriers, front, 14, 75, 103
celebrity baby match, 148
classes, 46, 51, 74, 167
cleaning services, 35
clothes, baby
    decorating with fabric paint, 104
    letting baby select, 115
    personalizing, 55, 68
    reselling, 157

sewing baby pants, 118–19
    slogans on, 117
    ugly clothes contest, 65
clothes, your, 26, 38, 82, 103, 134–35, 185
collage, initial, 204
conversation, 35, 79
cookies, making, 58
cooking meals ahead of time, 155
crawling race, 182
crocheting baby hats, 92
crying babies, 28, 40, 44

D

dancing, 180
dessert dates, 123
dog watching, 189
drive-through services, 73

E

e-mailing baby, 146
errands, 100, 164, 189
escaping solo, 167
exercise, 51, 88, 116

F

fabric paint, decorating with, 104

fabric stores, 71

family, 42, 149

farmer's markets, 112

farms, 181

fears, confronting, 72

feeding and changing places, scouting out, 23

feeding baby on the floor, 159

food, baby, 125, 127

food, ethnic, 54

food train, 50

footprints, painting on pottery, 32

formula, 26

friends

   game nights with, 166

   keeping in touch with, 28, 87

   listing mommy friends, 66

   meeting for errands, 164

   Mom's Night Out, 107

   movie/TV nights with, 106

   overnight getaway with, 99

   scheduling activities with, 96

   shopping with, 103

   talking to, 35

   TV nights with, 156

   walking in garden with, 97

G

game night, 166

gardens, botanical, 96

gear, 13, 198

getting out of the house, 3–4, 12, 158

gifts, 125, 130, 172, 197

Goodnight Moon, 200

graffiti, 171

grandparents, 15, 205

grocery shopping, 39, 69, 164

gyms, baby, 187, 199

H

handprints, finger paint, 153

hats, baby, 92

help, accepting, 113

hiking, 124, 184

hooky, playing, 165

hospital, driving by, 105

I

Inside-Outside parties, 158

Internet, using for errands, 100

J

jeans, interim, 38

jobs for babies, 137

K

knitting, 70

L

laundry baskets, 170

libraries, 94

lists, 17, 47, 71, 83

M

mall, 103, 158

Margarita Mommies Group, 173

massage, baby, 37

meals, 84, 98, 122

memory game, personalizing, 168

Mexican restaurants, 205

milkshakes, 196
moms, other, 30–31, 89,
    166, 179, 180, 195
movies, 28, 50, 73, 106, 128
museums, 64, 175, 187
music, 54, 91, 103, 167

N

needs, taking care of your
    own first, 18
new, trying something, 121
no, saying, 15

O

one-handed tasks, 29
online shopping, 100
outdoor stores, 198
overnight trips, 99, 205

P

pants, baby, 118–19
Paris, pretending to be in,
    24
partner
    acting like, 107
    communicating with, 83
    date with, 44
    dressing up for, 185
    encouraging time with

baby, 33
    holding hands with, 72
    jogging strollers for, 143
    making photo collage
        for, 92
    overnight trip with, 205
    showering with, 120
    surprising with a
        night out, 151
    taking care of baby, 66
    visiting at work, 48
planning solo escapes, 167
playing hooky from work, 165
pedicures, 49
pedometers, 46, 130
pet stores, 192
pets, letting baby ride, 86
phone, letting baby use, 186
photo books, 203
photo booth, 106
photographs
    baby contortionism, 143
    baby during walks, 55
    baby in different outfits,
        59
    baby in front of mirror,
        152
    baby with other children,
        124

baby's birthplace, 178
baby's obsession, 197
bad parenting examples,
    122
black and white, 102
collage of, 92
crying baby, 44
family photo wall, 149
feet, 39
graffiti as background, 171
monthly, 22
1-2-3 series, 178
professional, 125
putting into comic strip,
    87
putting on products, 76
security object, 188
sharing, 76
sleeping baby, 25
you with baby, 78
pickle spears, 169
picnics, 183
plant stores, 78
play dates, 155, 180
playthings, your old
    items as, 152
podcasts, 151
potluck dinner parties, 142
pubs, family-friendly, 136

purging your possessions, 138

purse, cleaning out, 94

R

rattles, making, 141

reading for pleasure, 67

research, letting baby participate in, 137

restaurants
    adult, 144
    brunch in, 128
    fast-food, 176
    Mexican, 205
    with partner and baby, 102
    takeout or delivery from, 32

resting, 66, 101

role playing, 131

running, 116

S

security objects, photographing, 188

sewing baby pants, 118–19

sex, 26, 53, 159

shell game, 199

shoes, 85, 147

shopping, 39, 56, 100, 103, 164

showering/bathing, 18, 64, 120, 132

sign language, baby, 140

singing, 59

sleeping late, 66

slides, 154

snow-day destinations, 182

spa day, 139

storage containers, plastic, 136

story times, 94, 164

strollers, jogging, 143

swimming, 57

swinging, 80

T

thank-you notes, personalizing, 85

time capsule, making, 21

touring your own town, 147

toy stores, 183

toys, 135, 165

tracking child's every movement, 20

trading cards, baby, 194

traditions, starting, 90

train game, 170

transportation, public, 172

treasure boxes, making, 172

TV, 82, 106, 156, 174

V

vegetables, introducing to baby, 112

videos of baby, 185, 190

volunteer work, 105

W

walking with baby, 12
    counting your steps, 46
    doubling your walk, 130
    for exercise, 116
    exploring new areas, 55
    in gardens, 96

water, drinking, 13

webcams, 89

wine-tasting party, 180

work, visiting people at, 48

writing, 52, 81, 83

Y

yes, saying, 113

yoga, 46

Z

zoos, 181, 202

Acknowledgments

Our first-borns, Julian and Holden, now impishly charming pre-schoolers, were once portable, snuggly infants who inspired this book. Thank you, boys.

Our second babies, Milo and Scarlett, field-tested these activities and sat quietly (sort of) in our laps as we typed up the manuscript.

Our husbands, Alec Flett and Ryan Currier, gave us incredible support and encouragement. You guys made it all happen (including the pregnancies).

Heather thanks Whitney for getting pregnant first. Whitney thanks Heather for jumping on the bandwagon. We both thank Gwyneth Paltrow for making motherhood cool.

We want to acknowledge the very special Sherry Reinhardt for connecting us with other new moms and instructing us to go on outings. She will be missed. We thank the women in our moms groups for cheering us on and joining us on our adventures, especially Laurie Schmitt, Erin McMahon, and Jeanine Strickland. Thanks to Sunny McKay for telling us about Berkeley moms groups and for confirming that we are not the only geeks who like to wear pedometers.

We thank the cleverest Sharon Schrank for suggesting the term *rookie mom*.

We are thankful for the enthusiasm and creativity of other parents who shared their activity ideas with us, especially Becky Senf, J. D. Griffoen, Maureen Layag, Molly Callender, Marla Murphy, Michelle Denk, Dr. Anne Mary Franks, and Dr. Bruce Linton.

Some wonderful friends acted as early readers. We are grateful to them for their tough love and thoughtful feedback: Heather Greenblum, Darci Rosenblum, Joanne Gouaux, Melissa Schwarz, Lisa Hazen, Olivia Harting, Heidi Swanson, Lisa Turner, and Crystal Yednak.

We thank the talented people at Quirk Books for turning our rookie book project into something tangible that can be chucked into a diaper bag. We single out Jason Rekulak (or maybe his wife) for deciding we were worthy and Melissa Wagner for bringing it all together.

Of course we thank people who gave us ugly baby clothes (see page 65).

Finally, we'd like to thank Julie from *The Love Boat* for being a role model.